LOW-SEW BOUTIQUE

Cheryl Weiderspahn

©2007 Cheryl Weiderspahn
Published by

kp **krause publications**
An Imprint of F+W Publications

700 East State Street • Iola, WI 54990-0001
715-445-2214 • 888-457-2873
www.krausebooks.com

Our toll-free number to place an order or obtain
a free catalog is 800-258-0929.

The following registered trademark terms and companies appear in this publication:
Bed Bath & Beyond®, Clover Bias Tape Maker by Clover Needlecraft, Conair, Dollar Tree®,
E6000® Glue by Eclectic Products, Fray Check™ Liquid Seam Sealant by Prym Dritz,
Gadgets and More, Hanes® Her Way, Lancôme Paris, Macy's way to shop®, Peltex by
Pellon®, Pier1®, Scotchgard™ Protector by 3M, Scrabble, Timtex™ Stabilizer by Timber
Lane Press, Wal-Mart, Williams-Sonoma™

Library of Congress Catalog Number: 2006935547

ISBN 13: 978-0-89689-434-1
ISBN 10: 0-89689-434-7

Designed by Rachael L. Knier
Edited by Tracy L. Conradt

Printed in China

ACKNOWLEDGMENTS

My heartfelt gratitude to:

My Krause Contacts,
  Candy Wiza, Acquisition Editor, who first invited me to submit a book proposal
  Maria Turner, my first editor
  Tracy Conradt, my second editor
  Susan Sliwicki, Quilting/Sewing Books Editorial Team Leader

My big sister, Marilyn, who is my on-the-road personal assistant, booth manager and main shopping accomplice (although we prefer to think of it as "retail research.")

My friend and webmaster, Gale, for emotional, spiritual and technical support at all hours of the day and night

My friend, Shirley, for always being available, no matter what

My friend, Sharon, for always believing in who I am and what I do

DEDICATION

This book is dedicated to the people whom I love and admire the most:

My parents, John and Opal Seber, who raised me by the old adage:
  Use it up,
  Wear it out,
  Make it do,
  Or do without.

My husband, Francis, who is endlessly supportive and would sacrifice anything for me.

Our children, Merideth and her husband Brad, and Nathan and his wife Barbara who teased me that my next book would probably be *101 Ways to Disguise Zucchini.*

Our granddaughter, Gracia, our little "Amazing Grace."

TABLE OF CONTENTS

INTRODUCTION

About the Artist

I am the youngest of five children. Mom and Dad were raised, married and started a family in the Great Depression and it had a profound effect on their inner fiber. Wastefulness was a crime. Mom saved everything. She was the original recycler. Dad was gifted with an engineering mind, which he passed on to all five of his children. In our home, it was second nature to make what you needed and you were encouraged to substitute whatever you could find to get the job done. It seldom dawned on me to use perfectly good money to buy what I wanted. Mom and Dad, now in their 90s, still giggle when I say "I come from good stock."

For as long as I can remember, nothing could suppress my creative nature. My fondest early childhood memories are related to forming something with my hands. Mom says she couldn't throw anything out because I would drag it out of the trash and make something out of it. The little black Featherweight became my best friend. Then Mom "upgraded" to a Singer Golden Touch and Sew, which never worked right, so I taught myself to repair sewing machines. I spent nine summers making elaborate 4-H sewing projects and won many coveted awards. During junior high, I faked sore throats to stay home to sew. I memorized the Simplicity, McCalls and Butterick catalogs every season, but seldom bought a pattern. The pictures in the catalogs were enough. I not only made everything I wore (including underwear), but was sewing for the public for pay on a regular basis from the time I was 12 years old.

As a young wife and mother on a dairy farm, my homemaking and mechanical skills were a matter of survival. With a devoted and loving, but overworked husband, two children, 300 acres, and almost 100 head of cows, something was always blowing up, shorting out, breaking down or falling over. Often it was me. Sewing was less an artistic expression and more a way to clothe my family, keep the household in good repair, make necessary gifts, and contribute a meager amount to the family income. More than 2,200 custom sewing jobs later (mostly huge drapery jobs and custom home decorating jobs), I was depressed, burned out and my sewing was going nowhere. I was so isolated on our rural dairy farm, and yearned to reach more women and satisfy my creative needs. Moving was not an option and I wanted to remain a stay-at-home Mom. Petitions for divine direction filled my days — but "I come from good stock." In time, launching Homestead Specialties Pattern Company (named after our 100 year old homestead) was the answer to my prayers. And, of course, you can wear every one of my practical clothing designs more than one way, up to 48 different ways in fact. Visit me at www.homesteadspecialties.com.

Even though the kids are grown and living on their own, I still can be found every evening in the barn with Francis doing chores. I love traveling about once a month to bring my pattern designs to you and now have exposure and opportunity to buy the best and most unique sewing supplies and tools in the entire nation. Now I sew because I want to, not because I have to. And I have discovered that writing, teaching and entertaining my new friends across the country is as fulfilling as designing and sewing.

One of my biggest thrills is finding something like a common soap dish on a clearance table, using it and some upholstery samples to make a drawstring purse and seeing the disbelief on my friends faces. (See this purse in the Gallery.) Nothing thrills me more than empowering you to do the same! Let me show you how to think outside the box, how to erase an object's intended purpose and see it as a component in a new design. Your own personal design! Let me show you how to see common functional items as things of beauty. You can make anything!

And my Mom and Dad and I will be so proud of you!

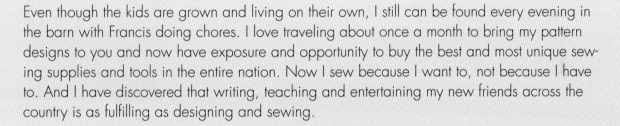

Cheryl Weiderspahn

CHAPTER 1
GETTING STARTED
Go Shopping!

Shopping? Yes! You love this book already, right? Every project in this book is created from at least one ready-made purchased kitchen textile. In this book, you will also find purse potential in other kitchen or common household items like cabinet handles and latches, napkin rings, tea strainers, egg timers, wooden spoons, feather dusters, a wooden hanger, necklaces, belts, key rings and chicken wire.

So go shopping! Shopping with a creative friend or two is often more successful because you will feed each other's creative tendencies and challenge yourselves to see who is first to recognize purse potential in everyday kitchen and household basics.

Over there, you spot an amazing place mat! Go ahead, pick it up and play with it. Turn it over in your hands. Fold it. Roll it up. Tuck it under your arm. Imagine it with straps. Put your hand inside and pretend to pull out your wallet. Ask it what it wants to be when it grows up. What other pieces coordinate with it? What can they be? Get the idea?

Look at these humble domestic basics in a new light. Erase their original intended purpose from your mind and see them as raw materials. Well, not exactly "raw" because they are pre-quilted and pre-lined; embroidered and embellished. They come with binding, beading, bangles and bells. Use these features to their fullest advantage. They give you a head start in the construction and do much of the work for you! You are on the fast track to boutique-worthy results.

Look for the obvious place mats, potholders and tea towels. But don't miss the possibilities in the coasters, soap dishes, table runners, oven mitts, trivets, tablecloths, curtains, rugs, cloth napkins, and even chair pads. You probably won't find the exact linens I used, but you may find even better ones! While you are at it, why not run over to the bed and bath aisle as well? Or the window treatments and home decor departments! Or fashion accessories!

Because your kitchen linens may vary in size from mine, you may have to slightly adjust the measurements given in the project instructions.

Where should you shop? Try department stores, discount stores and closeout outlets. Home furnishing stores like Ikea, Pottery Barn, Pier 1 Imports, Crate and Barrel, Bed Bath and Beyond, and Linens and Things are obvious choices. But don't pass up the stores where everything costs a dollar or even second-hand stores. Look at your small locally owned gift shops as well as chain gift shops, like the one at Cracker Barrel Restaurants. Kitchen gadget stores and restaurant suppliers are playgrounds as well. Your local fabric shop or quilt shop will yield great coordinating fabrics and supplies. You may even decide to make your own place mats from their fabric. Hardware and home improvement stores are some of my favorite playgrounds! Or go "shopping" in your own drawer of Great Grandmother's antique hand embroidered dresser scarves. The possibilities are endless!

One day after too much coffee, I was exploring purse possibilities at Home Depot. I wanted to privately peruse the plumbing, wiring, and various aisles, let my mind wonder, play with the merchandise, and wait for genius to strike. Inspiration kept getting interrupted by well-meaning employees offering to wait on me. After the fifth clerk offered his assistance, I finally blurted out, "Do you have any idea how I can turn that 15 horsepower air compressor into a pocketbook?" It worked! After that they left me alone!

GATHER YOUR TOOLS

You probably already have these sewing and crafting basics:

1 Sewing machine in good working order

2 Scissors, seam ripper

3 Rotary cutter, ruler and mat

4 Pins, hand sewing needles and size 90/14 or 100/16 sewing machine needles or jeans needles

5 Air-erase or water-erase fabric marking pens

6 Iron and ironing board

7 Screwdriver (either Phillips or slotted) for the kitchen cabinet handles on Summer Classic and the 9 to 5 Briefcase

8 Needle nose pliers/wire cutters for the chicken wire on The Three Minute Egg Purse

Buy more sewing machine needles than you think you will need. Breakage is common when sewing heavy layers. Jeans or Denim Needles are sharper and more slender than regular machine needles. They penetrate heavy fabrics without hesitation.

TIPS, TOOLS AND TECHNIQUES

Stitching Tips for Success

Even though these projects are low-sew, there are a few sewing tips you need to know:

1 Buy high-quality all-purpose thread. Polyester thread has good tensile strength and comes in many colors.

2 Slow down! Listen to your machine! It cannot ram through heavy layers at top speed.

3 Backstitch at the beginning and end of every seam.

4 Any seams under a lot of stress or bearing a lot of weight should be stitched twice for strength. It is so much easier to stitch it twice now than to repair it later.

5 Most of the machine stitching in this book is a simple straight stitch. The instructions will tell you if it is wrong sides together or right sides together.

6 "Topstitching" simply means to stitch from the top. This stitching line will show on top of the finished project.

7 Some of the projects need raw edges serged or zigzagged. This is to prevent fraying. Liquid seam sealant can also be used for small areas. I prefer to use Fray Check by Dritz.

8 The rug totes and Weekender Collection have instructions for a wide multiple stitch zigzag to join butted edges.

9 All handstitching in this book is done with a doubled thread.

10 If your sewing machine protests at the thicknesses, take those seams to your local upholstery shop or use glue.

Glue

Some seams are too thick to be sewn by your sewing machine. Don't stress your machine! Join the layers with a bead of E6000 or a rubber cement type glue, then clamp with wooden pinch-type clothespins or weight with a pile of books until the glue is set. I always wait at least 24 hours for the glue to cure before using the purse. You will not be able to change your mind after the glue is set! But, if you get it on your hand, just rub and it will fall off. It is machine washable and dryable, but not dry cleanable.

Fusible Interfacing, Stabilizers or Batting

Depending on the weight of your purchased textiles, and depending on the desired stiffness/body, you may need to add a layer of fusible interfacing, stabilizer or batting, even if the directions do not call for it. Peltex and Timtex work well as interfacing. Boning (like you sew into a strapless dress) can be used to support a weak edge and is easy to sew through.

Spray Basting Adhesive

This is used to control layers without pins. Protect surrounding area from over-spray and use good ventilation. Just spray and pat the layers together. Layers can be peeled apart and repositioned. This spray won't gum up your needle. (OK, here is my off-the-wall hint for using Spray Basting Adhesive: One day at a sewing expo, I simply could not keep my bra straps up. I was scheduled to present a style show on stage and knew that no one would consider me much of a fashion authority if they noticed my dilemma. A quick spray on each shoulder solved my problem for the rest of the day.)

1" Bias Tape Maker

I use the Clover Bias Tape Maker and this little tool is worth its weight in gold. With a bias tape maker you are able to make your own bias or straight grain binding. It will be helpful and timesaving for the Quilted Scarf in Chapter 5, the belt loops for Head for the Beach in Chapter 2 and several projects for the Weekender Collection in Chapter 6.

Magnetic Snaps

These snaps are another one of my favorite notions. We have been enjoying these for years on ready made purses, but only recently have been able to buy them to use on our projects. They make a professional-looking and secure closure. A set is comprised of male and female halves and a washer for the back of each. Although these come in several sizes, ¾" is the size used in this book. Using the accompanying washer as a template, make two small slits in the fabric slightly smaller than the prongs. Slide prongs through fabric. If your fabric is loosely woven or lightweight, use a reinforcing square of fabric, then push the washer over the prongs on the back. With your fingers, firmly push prongs toward each other to overlap, or push them apart. No tools are needed if your fingers are strong.

Zippers

Few things strike fear in the heart of a sewer like inserting a zipper and buttonholes. (There are no buttonholes in this entire book.) Those of you suffering from zipper-phobia can take heart. Every zipper in this project is simply topstitched on a finished edge, often on the right side so you can see what you are doing! No pre-basting the opening closed first, no lapped applications, no tricky techniques. Trust me!

Metal Eyelets

Metal eyelets or grommets are used to reinforce drawstring or cord in Faux Leather Backpack and Asian-Inspired Backpack in Chapter 4 and the Luggage Tag in Chapter 6. Metal eyelets are more durable than button holes under the abrasion of a drawstring. They consist of two nesting parts crimped together with a hammer and come in several finishes and sizes. Apply them according to the manufacturer's directions.

A woman in her lifetime will spend far more hours hugging a handbag than a man.

—*Ellen Rachlin, American poet*

Fabric Protector

This is the single most important thing you can use to keep your project looking newer and cleaner longer. Use good ventilation. Do not spray leather, vinyl, satin or fur. Retreat after laundering. I prefer Scotchgard Fabric Protector.

Note: Some kitchen textiles already have a stain release finish. Test it by spritzing with water and waiting a minute. If it beads up and rolls off, it is probably treated. If it soaks in, it is not treated, so treat it yourself.

CHAPTER 2

TEEN AND 'TWEEN MINI PURSES

Mini Purses are appealing to a teen or 'tween (age 8 to 12; that stage 'tween being a child and teenager). This up-to-date youthful trio can be low-sew projects for you or learn-to-sew projects for a young person in your life.

Cheryl's tips for teaching teens

Crafting, embellishing and sewing are in style and 'tweens and teens are passionate about it. Help your young person discover the joy of making something from nothing. Let them pick out their own favorite trendy colors. Together, examine ready-mades they love and discuss how you can duplicate them at home. Keep goals attainable so they experience the joy of completion. Keep it light and easygoing. Never force-feed a sewing lesson. Self esteem is far more important than a straight seam. Encourage always. Let them own their own sewing tools and provide a cool tote to store them. Let them catch you bragging to your friends about what a great job they are doing and how proud you are. Place them in front of a mirror wearing or holding the finished project, hold them by the shoulders and praise them till they glow!

HEAD FOR THE BEACH

Level of Difficulty

Gone fishing? Fishing for compliments that is. You are sure to catch a bucket-full of compliments with the sassy simplicity of this tiny tote. It is quickly fashioned from a potholder that has a pocket (to slide your hand into when removing hot dishes from the oven). The loop is already on the purchased potholder; just add a handmade shell button to finish the closure. The shell necklace-turned-handle can be tucked inside the purse if not needed. Then slide your belt through both belt loops on the back and it is a hands-free belt purse. Don't let this one get away!

Ingredients for this recipe

- Rectangular pocket potholder with loop
- 36" shell necklace
- 2" x 5" piece coordinating fabric for two belt loops
- Glue-on button shank
- Sea shell
- Glue
- Matching thread
- Optional: 1" Clover Bias Tape Maker for the belt loops

Instructions

Fold line

Front of potholder

1 Fold top of potholder down to form purse flap. Mark fold line with pins.

Binding

Fold line

Belt loops

Back of potholder

2 Fold and press fabric for belt loops so that both long raw edges meet in the middle. Fold in half (it is now ½" wide) and topstitch all four edges. Cut in half to make two belt loops. Turn ends under ½" and pin. Topstitch belt loops below fold line on back of potholder.

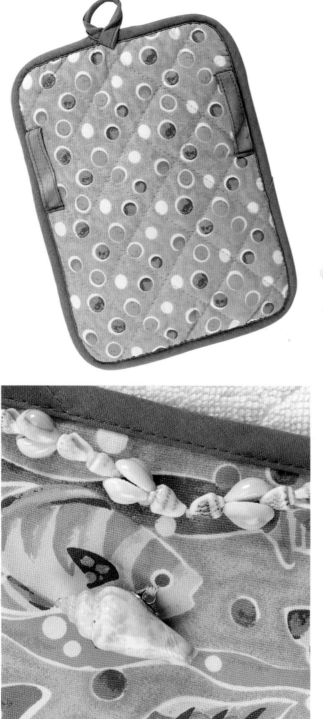

3 Handstitch necklace under flap. Let the stitches fall between the shells to hide them.

4 Choose a sea shell that fits through the button loop. To make button, glue the button shank to the shell. Let glue set. Fold down flap to determine placement for button. Sew on button.

These glue-on button shanks can turn almost anything into a button or sew-on embellishment. Glue to the back of tumbled glass or stone, sea shell, coin, bead, Scrabble tile, charm or trinket, puzzle piece, doll house miniature or any found item. I have had rare antique buttons that were no longer useable because the original shank broke off. You guessed it, I repaired them with a new glue-on shank.

OUT OF THE BLUE

Level of Difficulty

We witness breathtaking sunsets from our vantage point on our hill-top farm. As the sun sinks behind our corn fields, it is tousled with scarlet, purple and peach. The fringe on "Out of the Blue" is tousled with the same colors. The purse is made from two sky-colored potholders joined on three sides. Use the potholders' hanging loops to hold the handle, and this purse is made in minutes! A true blue friend.

Ingredients for this recipe

- (2) 8" blue quilted square potholders with hanging loops*
- ¾" silver magnetic snap
- ½ yd. fringe trim
- 1½ yd. denim trim for strap
- Matching thread
- Glue
- 8 pinch-type clothespins
- * Potholders used in this project were purchased at Ikea.

Instructions

1 Lay out potholders with both hanging loops in upper left corners. The hanging loops will later be used to attach the shoulder strap.

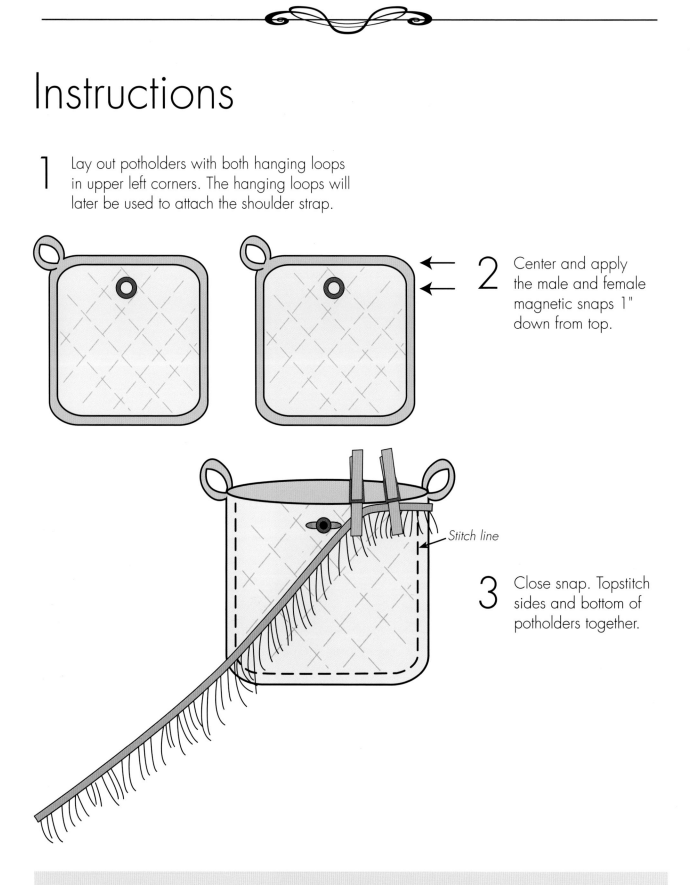

2 Center and apply the male and female magnetic snaps 1" down from top.

Stitch line

3 Close snap. Topstitch sides and bottom of potholders together.

This bag is so small that it can be worn as a hidden security pouch under your clothing while traveling to hide your passport, jewelry and extra money.

4   Glue fringe to top of purse and clamp with clothespins until glue is set. The fringe hides the snap prongs.

5   Loop denim trim through both potholder loops and stitch or glue to secure.

FIREFLIES

Level of Difficulty

As the summer sun sets, the fireflies emerge in all their sparkling splendor. Remember chasing fireflies into a quart canning jar, capping it with a lid with holes, and setting it on your night stand for a twinkling night light? Well, now it is your night to shine carrying this sparkling purse.

Ingredients for this recipe

- 2 square potholders
- 2 ⅞" buttons
- 30" beaded necklace with hook closure for handle
- 3" tassel
- ¾" gold magnetic snap
- Matching thread

Ok, confession time. I really didn't purchase these potholders. You probably already figured that out anyway. You knew the metallic threads would melt on a hot dish. But I fell in love with the place mats and made potholder-sized squares out of them to make this purse.

Instructions

1 Measure to determine center of purse sides. Add 1" above center of purse sides and join points and mark fold lines with pins.

2 Center and apply the male and female magnetic snaps 1" down from fold lines.

3 Close snap. Topstitch sides and bottom of potholders together, enclosing top loop of tassel in the seam.

4 Fold down flap on fold line and hand sew button in place to tack flap down. The flap hides the snap prongs.

5 Handstitch necklace ends to top of purse to form handle.

CHAPTER 3
POSH PURSES

Stir up a quick batch of these by simply using rugs or place mats. The optional handles can be made from beaded belts and necklaces or unexpected finds such as kitchen cabinet hardware. It takes just minutes to make — it will take more time to shop for the supplies than to sew! These low-sew recipes yield boutique-worthy results quickly and economically!

"I find that it is vital to have at least one handbag for each of the ten social occasions: Very Formal, Not So Formal, Just a Teensy Bit Formal, Informal But Not That Informal, Every Day, Every Other Day, Day Travel, Night Travel, Theatre and Fling."
— Miss Piggy

GLITZ AND GLAM

Level of Difficulty

Never did a dollar store place mat, a beaded napkin ring and a few minutes at the sewing machine yield such luxurious results! This purse is romantic and polished enough for the bride's essentials on her special day, yet classic enough for any elegant occasion.

Ingredients for this recipe

- Rectangular ivory satin brocade place mat with angled corners*
- 2" beaded napkin ring**
- 22" x 1" satin ribbon
- Matching thread
- * Place mat used in this project was purchased at Dollar Tree.
- ** Napkin ring used in this project was purchased at Bed Bath and Beyond.

Instructions

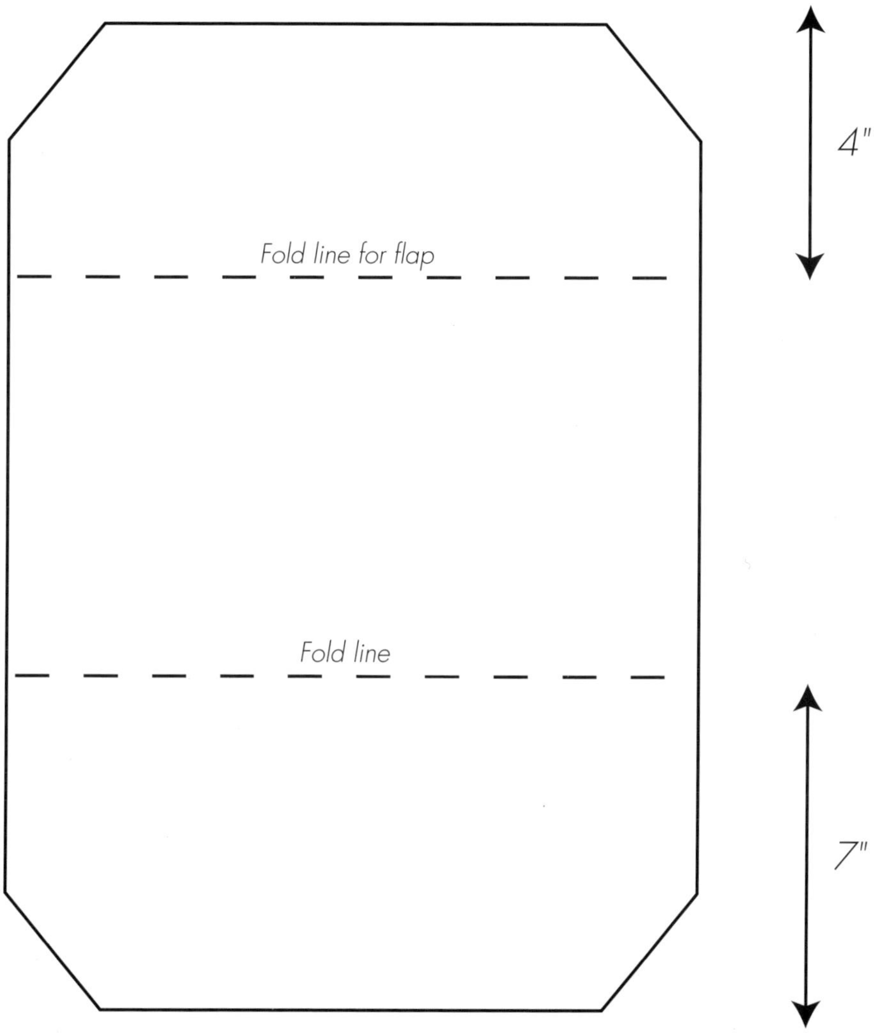

Fold line for flap

Fold line

4"

7"

1 Measure and mark
fold lines with pins.

2 Fold bottom of purse up and topstitch sides together.

3 Center and handstitch napkin ring, extending over the edge of the flap. Let the stitches fall between the beads to hide them.

4 Stitch center of ribbon to purse front under napkin ring. To close the purse, bring the ribbon ends around the napkin ring and tie in a pretty bow.

FUNKY AND FUN-LOVING

This casual fun-loving summer bag is so easy to make, you can complete it in the morning before the sun comes out. It will be begging you to grab it and go out for a day of adventure in the sun.

Ingredients for this recipe

- Rectangular vinyl straw-looking place mat*
- Bead necklace or bead belt with hook closure for handle
- (2) 1" key rings (split rings)
- 1" wood bead for closure
- 12" tan rayon cord or braid to attach bead and to make button loop
- 10" of ½" tan grosgrain ribbon to cover boning and ends of button loop
- 6" of boning (stays)
- Matching thread
- * Place mat used in this project was purchased at Bed Bath and Beyond.

When shopping for a natural straw, rattan or raffia place mat, test it by folding it. Is it too stiff to bend? Will fibers break if you crease it? Worse yet, some place mats are actually made of woven paper and are not washable and will not wear well. Vinyl look-alikes will perform much better.

Instructions

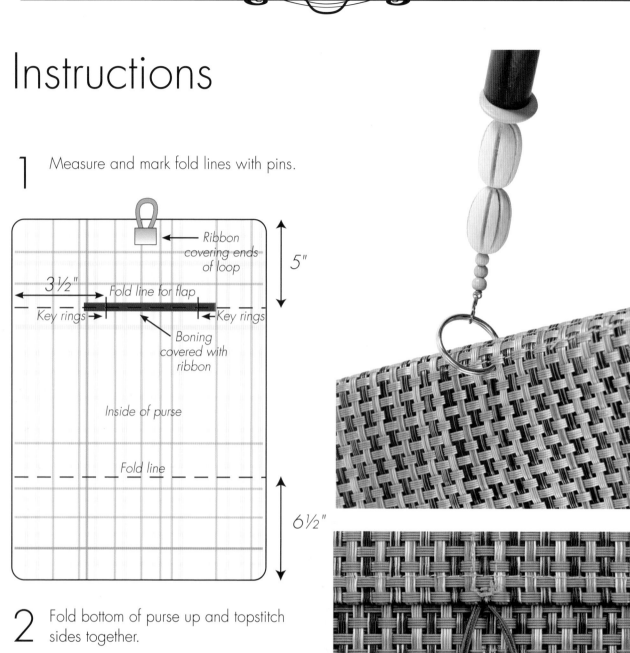

1 Measure and mark fold lines with pins.

Ribbon covering ends of loop

5"

3½"

Fold line for flap

Key rings → | ← Key rings

Boning covered with ribbon

Inside of purse

Fold line

6½"

2 Fold bottom of purse up and topstitch sides together.

3 Center and topstitch boning to the wrong side of the place mat in the fold line for flap. Cut ribbon to 7" and fold ends over. Center over boning, stitch around ribbon to cover. Loop key rings through place mat and around boning 3½" in from ends. The boning helps give the bag shape and support when carried by the handle. Hook necklace to key rings.

4 Fold 4" of rayon cord in half and hand-stitch ends together. Center and stitch to back of flap.

5 Fold ends under on remaining ribbon and stitch on top of loop cord ends to cover.

6 Loop remaining rayon cord through bead and thread through front of purse and tie inside purse.

SUMMER CLASSIC

This otherwise conservative and image-conscious envelope bag has an innovative twist. (You know, there is an overachiever hidden in all of us!) Its classic gold trim spent its first life as kitchen cabinet hardware! So go ahead, get a handle on it, and make one today!

Ingredients for this recipe

- Rectangular vinyl straw and brocade place mat*
- Matching thread
- Brass kitchen cabinet handle
- Matching brass cabinet back plate
- (2) 8-32 by ½" truss head or pan head machine bolts (slotted or Phillips head)

- Brass hook and staple closure (hobby hardware aisle at the hardware or home improvement store)
- ¼" brass bead to attach hook
- (4) ³⁄₁₆" brass beads to attach staple
- * Place mat used in this project was purchased at Wal-Mart.

Instructions

1 Measure and mark fold lines with pins.

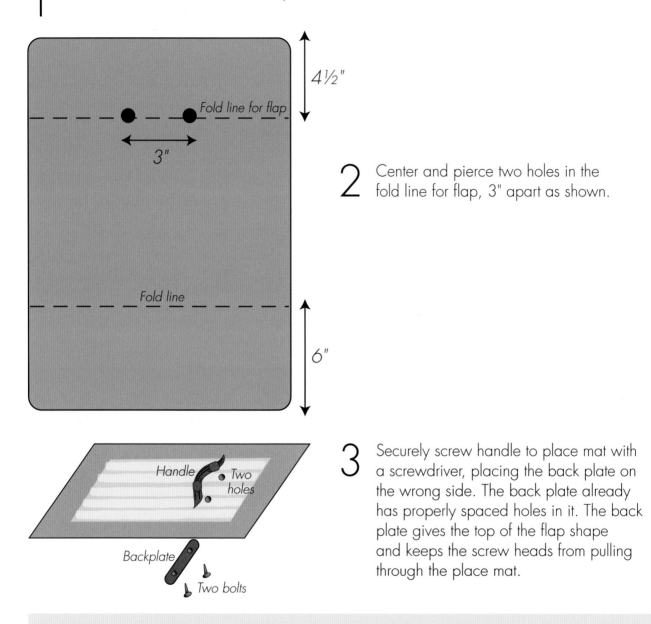

4½"

Fold line for flap

3"

Fold line

6"

2 Center and pierce two holes in the fold line for flap, 3" apart as shown.

Handle

Two holes

Backplate

Two bolts

3 Securely screw handle to place mat with a screwdriver, placing the back plate on the wrong side. The back plate already has properly spaced holes in it. The back plate gives the top of the flap shape and keeps the screw heads from pulling through the place mat.

The two screws that come with your cabinet handle are too long. They are designed to go through a wood cabinet door and you are only going through a thin place mat. So here is the plan. March right into the hardware store with your head held high. You won't need a cart. Find the cabinet handle you love and the coordinating back plate in the same aisle. With a confident voice, ask the fellow who offers to wait on you for the two bolts in the ingredients list. You will follow him to a wall of tiny drawers. He will decipher the code on the drawers and drop two little bolts into a little plastic bag on which he will write the price (under 50 cents for both of them). He may even offer to test screw them into the handle you are holding. Pay at the cash register and you are home free! How empowering!

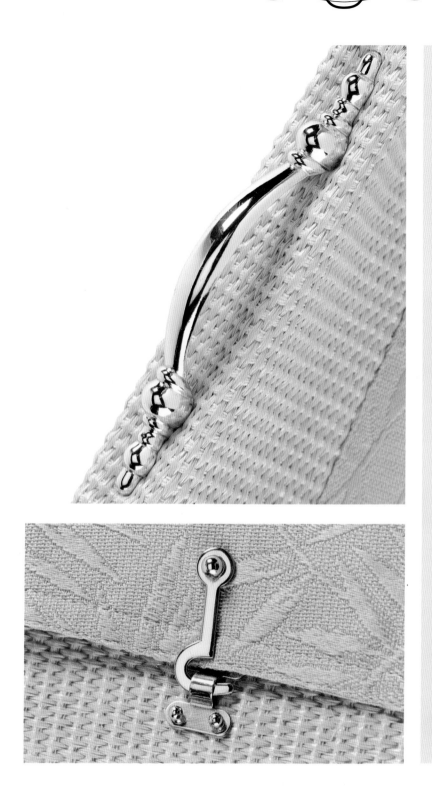

One summer day while stacking bales of hay in the hay mow of our 115 year old barn, I happened across a nest of about nine kittens. The nest was just a burrowed-out dish in the hay no bigger than the inside of one of these envelope purses. The odd thing was that these kittens were from two different litters. I estimated them to be about a week to ten days apart in age. I kept an eye on the nest from a distance for the next week or two and this is what I discovered. Both mothers were taking shifts to co-parent that blended family! One mother would leave to hunt and have some time off while the other mother would stay home and protect and nurse the entire brood. Without saying a word, these two single mothers had struck a mutually beneficial agreement.

- No feasibility study or start-up loan
- No employee criminal background checks or drug tests
- No zoning laws, building permit or safety inspection of the work site
- No liability insurance or heath care coverage
- No resume, job description, contract or periodic performance review
- No time clock, work schedule or minimum care-giver to infant ratio

Just two rural neighbor ladies with similar needs who came to each other's aid. I wish our lives could be that simple.

4 Fold place mat up and topstitch sides together.

5 Handstitch the hook and staple closure to close the flap. Do not use the nails or screws that come with the hardware. Sew from the back of the place mat, up through the screw hole in the hardware and through a brass bead, back down through the same screw hole and to the back of the place mat. Repeat this several times in each hole.

ETHNIC INTRIGUE

Level of Difficulty

The intrigue of textured faux leather and rich earthy beads are pulled from an untamed exotic culture. Hear the tribal drums and wild animals in the distance?

Ingredients for this recipe

- Rectangular pieced faux leather place mat*
- 1½" x 1" rectangular button
- 1" x ⅝" rectangular button
- 2" of beaded fringe in natural colors
- 5" of beaded fringe in red
- ¾" gold magnetic snap

- Matching thread
- Glue
- 4 pinch-type clothespins
- * Place mat used in this project was purchased at Pier 1 Imports.

Instructions

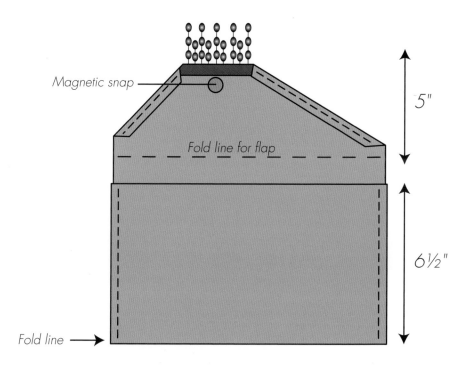

Magnetic snap

Fold line for flap

Fold line →

5"

6½"

1 Measure and mark fold lines.

2 Fold up and topstitch sides together.

3 Fold corners of flap back, following the lines of the piecing as a guide. Topstitch along these folds. Trim excess off under flap.

4 Stitch the 5" piece of beaded fringe to the bottom of the flap.

5 Apply the male magnetic snap portion to flap.

6 Stack and glue buttons together. Glue 2" piece of beaded fringe to back of large button. Glue this button and bead medallion to the front of the flap to cover prongs of magnetic snap. Let glue set. Apply remaining female half of magnetic snap to purse front.

SASSY CHIC

Dangerously red nail polish, lipstick, pumps and matching clutch. No well-dressed diva would be caught without these essentials! This sophisticated clutch will really get their attention if you confess that you made it yourself. The hardest part was picking out the button for the closure!

Ingredients for this recipe

- Rectangular red faux leather place mat*
- 1" beaded button
- 4" red rayon cord for button loop
- 2½" red grosgrain ribbon to cover ends of button loop
- Matching thread
- * Place mat used in this project was purchased at Bed Bath and Beyond.

Instructions

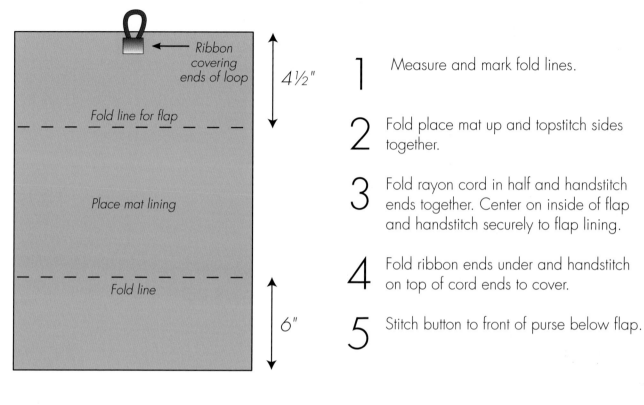

Ribbon covering ends of loop

4½"

Fold line for flap

Place mat lining

Fold line

6"

1 Measure and mark fold lines.

2 Fold place mat up and topstitch sides together.

3 Fold rayon cord in half and handstitch ends together. Center on inside of flap and handstitch securely to flap lining.

4 Fold ribbon ends under and handstitch on top of cord ends to cover.

5 Stitch button to front of purse below flap.

THE CHAMELEON PURSE

Level of Difficulty

Cleverly changing colors to match its surroundings, the Chameleon Purse can adapt to any outfit. By shedding its outer layer (slipcovers simply made from place mats), you have the versatility of many looks in one unique bag! The matching change purse is made by sewing a zipper to two crocheted coasters. A charming heart-shaped tea strainer locket is the 'jewelry' that completes the ensemble.

Ingredients for this recipe

- 4 assorted embellished place mats for slipcovers (all the same size)*
- 2 coordinating napkins (at least 20" square) or ¾ yd. of medium-weight pink fabric plus ¾ yd. of medium-weight blue fabric for base purse
- Matching thread
- 4 yd. of ¾" wide hook-and-loop fastener
- Silver heart-shaped tea strainer**

- Silver purse handle with removable rods and detachable shoulder chain
- 2 crocheted coasters for change purse
- Matching zipper for change purse, minimum 16"
- Zipper pull for change purse, optional
- * Place mats and napkins used in this project were purchased at Macy's Department Store.
- ** Tea strainers were purchased at Gadgets and More.

Instructions

MAKE THE REVERSIBLE BASE PURSE

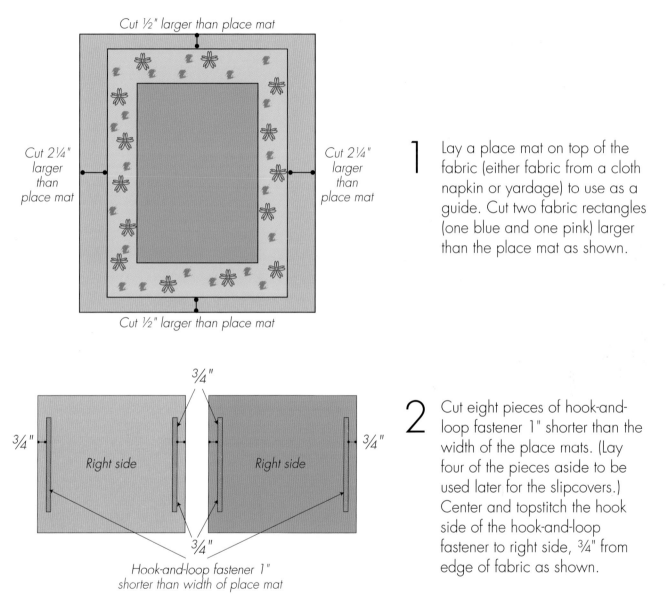

Cut ½" larger than place mat

Cut 2¼" larger than place mat

Cut 2¼" larger than place mat

Cut ½" larger than place mat

1 Lay a place mat on top of the fabric (either fabric from a cloth napkin or yardage) to use as a guide. Cut two fabric rectangles (one blue and one pink) larger than the place mat as shown.

¾"

¾"

¾"

Right side

Right side

¾"

Hook-and-loop fastener 1" shorter than width of place mat

2 Cut eight pieces of hook-and-loop fastener 1" shorter than the width of the place mats. (Lay four of the pieces aside to be used later for the slipcovers.) Center and topstitch the hook side of the hook-and-loop fastener to right side, ¾" from edge of fabric as shown.

If your cloth napkins are not quite big enough, remove the stitching from the napkin hems, unfold and press flat to make more space.

The interior of a bag is a very private space. One of the more unattractive gestures a man can make is thrusting his hand into a woman's purse.

—Amy Fine Collins, Special Correspondent, Vanity Fair

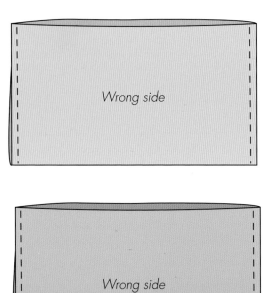

Wrong side

Wrong side

3 Fold fabric rectangles in half, right sides together, and stitch sides with a ½" seam allowance. Press seams open.

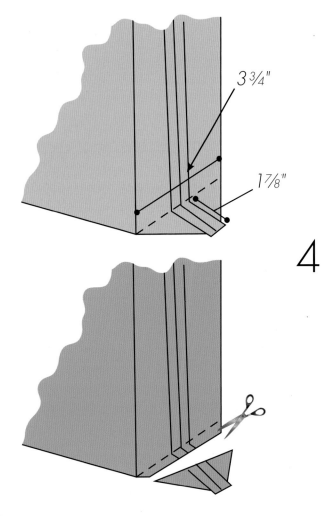

3¾"

1⅞"

4 To box the bottom corners of the purse, fold and stitch as shown. Trim seam to ½" seam allowance.

5 To make the rod pockets for the handles, cut two pieces of blue fabric and two pieces of pink fabric, each measuring 7¼" x 2". Seam together with a ½" seam allowance. Press seams open.

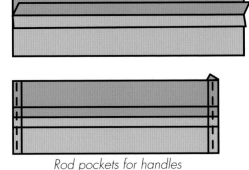

6 Serge or zigzag short raw ends. Press under ends ½" and topstitch.

Rod pockets for handles

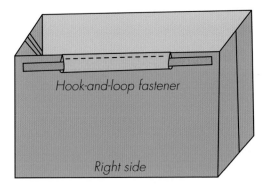

Hook-and-loop fastener

Right side

7 Fold both rod pocket strips in half along seam, with right sides out, and press. Center and pin to top of purse, placing raw edges even and right sides together. Stitch in place with a ½" seam allowance.

8 Fold under the top raw edges ½" on both purses and press. The rod pockets will now extend above the top of the purse. With one purse right-side out and the other wrong-side out, nest purses with wrong sides together, matching side seams. Join by topstitching together along top, stitching close to the edge. Your base purse is reversible and can be used with the blue side out or the pink side out.

9 Attach handle by inserting rods through handles and rod pockets and securing with nuts. Attach optional shoulder chain.

10 Clip tea strainer to handle.

Because these handles are removable and interchangeable, they can be used on a variety of different fabric bags! This one handle kit can be the basis for an entire wardrobe of fabulous bags!

Cut and glue two photos to fit inside the tea strainer and it becomes a locket!

MAKE THE PLACE MAT SLIPCOVERS

1 Center and topstitch the loop side of the hook-and-loop fastener ¼" from edge of four place mats as shown. Your slipcovers are done.

MAKE THE CHANGE PURSE

1 Open zipper. Topstitch zipper all around edges of coasters as shown, stitching close to edges.

Wrong side of coasters

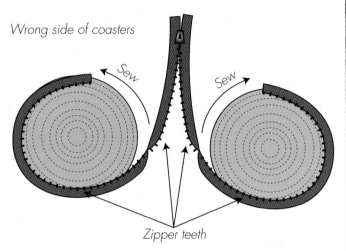

Sew

Sew

Zipper teeth

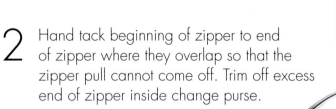

2 Hand tack beginning of zipper to end of zipper where they overlap so that the zipper pull cannot come off. Trim off excess end of zipper inside change purse.

3 Attach zipper pull if desired.

THREE MINUTE EGG PURSE

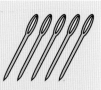

What a head-turning conversation purse! Don't take life so seriously! Fry one up for yourself! This bag is garnished with an egg timer and wooden spoons that hatched into handles. Real chicken wire gives the purse its shape. See the poor fellow peering out from his wire cage? Your friends will be clucking and chuckling at your witty and whimsical tongue-in-cheek (or tongue-in-beak?) creation at your next hen party! They will consider you one hot chick!

Ingredients for this recipe

- Rectangular chicken place mat for purse front and back*
- Coordinating chicken napkin (or ½ yd. of chicken print fabric)*
- 2 coordinating fringed checked napkins or ½ yd. checked fabric
- Batting or craft fleece, 4" x 45"
- Matching thread
- 1½ yd. of 1" chicken wire (the correct name is 1" poultry netting) from the feed store or hardware store
- Duct tape
- 2 slotted wooden spoons for handles*
- Wooden hourglass-style egg timer*
- 2 glue-on button shanks
- Tassel made of feathers
- 12" rayon cord
- Spray basting adhesive
- Glue
- 4 pinch-type clothespins
- Needle nose pliers
- * Items used in this project were purchased at Williams Sonoma.

I was unable to find a feather tassel while shopping in our rural area. So I swiped some choice feathers from my ostrich feather duster and glued them up into two wooden beads. Viola!

Instructions

PREPARE THE PLACE MATS

1 Prepare chicken place mat by cutting in half. Half of the place mat will be the purse front and the other half will be the purse back.

2 Turn raw edges of place mat to the inside and topstitch closed.

MAKE THE GUSSET

1 Measure around three sides of the front or back purse piece. This is the length of the gusset. Cut the following pieces (the napkins will have to be pieced to attain the required length):

A Using a wire cutters, cut a piece of chicken wire 3" wide by the length of the gusset. With needle nose pliers, tuck any wire ends in and away from the edge so that they do not poke through the fabric. Sharp ends may be covered with tiny pieces of duct tape to cushion them and protect fabric.

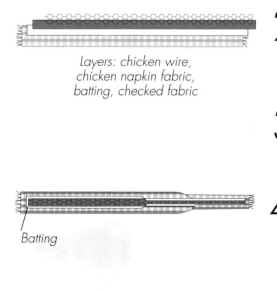

B Cut a piece of chicken napkin or chicken fabric 3" wide by the length of the gusset. If possible, position chicken's heads so that they appear to be peering through their wire cage.

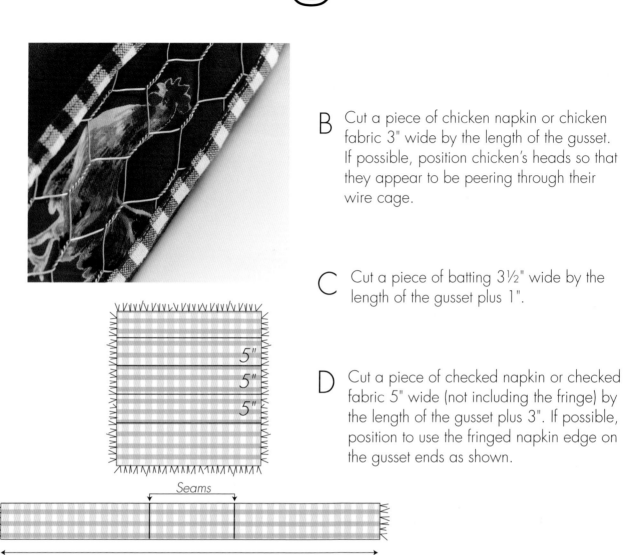

5"

5"

5"

Seams

Gusset length plus 3" (not including fringe)

C Cut a piece of batting 3½" wide by the length of the gusset plus 1".

D Cut a piece of checked napkin or checked fabric 5" wide (not including the fringe) by the length of the gusset plus 3". If possible, position to use the fringed napkin edge on the gusset ends as shown.

Layers: chicken wire, chicken napkin fabric, batting, checked fabric

2 Center and layer these gusset pieces in the order shown. Use spray basting adhesive to keep the layers centered.

3 Wrap the batting over the sides of the chicken wire ¼". Baste in place.

Batting

4 Turn under the checked fabric edge ½" and pin. Wrap the checked fabric over the top of the chicken wire ½". Hand or machine stitch in place through all the layers. If machine stitching, stitch slowly and take care to not let the needle break by landing directly on the chicken wire.

ASSEMBLE THE PURSE

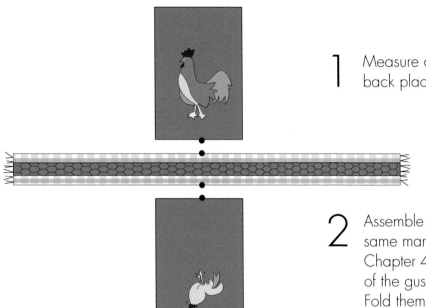

1 Measure and mark center of front and back place mats and gusset.

2 Assemble front and back to gusset in the same manner as the 9 to 5 Briefcase in Chapter 4, page 57. The fringed ends of the gusset will extend up on each side. Fold them down to the outside of the purse and handstitch in place.

ATTACH THE WOODEN SPOON HANDLES

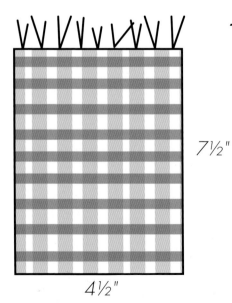

7½"

4½"

1 Cut four tabs, 4½" x 7½" from the other checked napkin. Position fringed edge of napkin on ends of tabs.

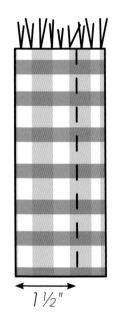

1½"

2 The following instructions will make tabs 1½" wide. You may have to adjust for the slot size of your spoons. Fold tabs in half and stitch as shown. Press seam allowances open and turn right side out. Press. Serge or zigzag raw edges on unfringed end of tab.

3 Topstitch tabs to the top of place mats. Spacing will depend on your spoon and place mat size. Slide tabs through slots in spoons and stitch fringed ends to front of purse.

If you are unable to find spoons with a slot in the handle, check with your local finish carpenter, cabinet or furniture making shop to see if a slot can be cut. Or simply let the tab go over the top of the spoon handle and tack in place with rubber cement glue so it cannot slide off.

EMBELLISH WITH EGG TIMER AND FEATHER TASSEL JUST FOR FUN

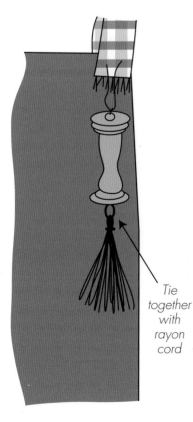

Tie together with rayon cord

1 Center and attach glue-on button shanks to top and bottom of egg timer with glue. Let glue set.

2 Cut rayon cord in half. Assemble egg timer and tassel as shown with rayon cord. Tuck cord ends up under a tab and stitch or glue in place.

Speaking of farming. . . .

A True Story about How Cows Embellish Your Clothes

Helping deliver calves is one of the most rewarding jobs on the dairy farm. The miracle of birth is always new and wondrous.

One such "blessed event" stands out in my mind more than the others. On one hot summer afternoon a few years ago, we were calling cows to come in for evening milking. One cow didn't come in with the rest of the herd. Now it was my job to go round up the stray cows, and since our Border Collie never figured out how, I was the family dog.

I found "Josie" (names have been changed to protect the innocent) a half-mile from the barn in an advanced stage of labor. It was her first calf and her big brown eyes pleaded for an epidural. At the risk of being too graphic, let me just say that I knew the calf was in trouble and that it needed to be pulled into the world and get oxygen soon.

I must explain that Josie didn't even belong to us. We were boarding her for friends. Josie was their 10 year old's 4-H project. So I was understandably overwhelmed with the responsibility of saving both mother and child. I just couldn't deal with causing someone else's 10-year old son to cry. Yet my options were few.

PLAN A: Taking Matters Into My Own Hands (literally)
Now I've pulled lots of calves before, but usually with latex gloves. Well, this particular pasture was plum out of latex gloves. Deep breath. I grasped a slimy wet calf hoof in each hand and pulled hard. This landed me flat on my bottom, right where Josie's water had broken earlier in the day. This is when the embellishment started.

PLAN B: Yankee Ingenuity
No paper towels in this pasture. (Will somebody please start a grocery list?) No baler twine lying around either. (Farmers are famous for fixing things with baler twine.) I wiped my hands on my shorts (more embellishment) and picked handfuls of weeds and wiped off the calf's ankles, tightened my grip and pulled again. Still not enough traction, but at least I stayed on my feet this time.

PLAN C: Using What Is On Hand
It's summer, no socks to slide over my hands to use as gloves. Just my T-shirt and shorts. No time to run back to the barn. In my panic, I voted for the shorts.

Timing my pulls with Josie's heaves, my brain scrambled to remember what I learned in Lamaze class 13 years earlier. Eventually we triumphantly welcomed a 100-pound healthy heifer calf into the world! I tickled its nose with a stick to make it start breathing while Josie licked it clean. Our bonding and maternal afterglow was soon interrupted by the stark realization that I was grievously under-dressed for the occasion! From the waist down my fashion faux pas consisted of merely Hanes Her Way and dusty tennis shoes!

I was just yards from the road, but a half-mile from the barn. No high weeds or trees to hide behind. No Plan D and the Mennonite Wednesday evening pilgrimage to mid-week prayer meeting would soon be parading past. I could stand behind Josie to hide, but that would only be a temporary fix. Yet, I was not putting those shorts back on. I do have some pride. So I just ran as fast as I could, scanning up and down the road, yanking my T-shirt down as far as it would go, which was not nearly far enough.

I figured I'd earned a Hero's Homecoming back in the barn for my sacrificial act. But instead, Hubby and Son thought my lack of proper attire was the funniest thing they had ever seen. Amid their uncontrolled laughter, I wrapped a feedbag around myself and headed to the house to change clothes to finish chores. Some thanks I get.

CHAPTER 4
TOTALLY TOTES

Any of the bags in this chapter can be used for a variety of purposes. You could use one of the rug totes for a diaper bag or gym bag. Besides being large, they are washable and very durable. Or, make a fashionable backpack to coordinate with your clothing. For a professional but inexpensive briefcase, the 9 to 5 Briefcase can fill that need. Use your imagination with any of these bags and your friends will be asking, "Where did you get that?"

9 TO 5 BRIEFCASE

Level of Difficulty

This is a stylish and professional-looking bag for a business engagement, class or carrying your laptop. Its clean lines lend a bit of polished up-scale sophistication. The crowning touch is a kitchen cabinet handle! No one will guess you made it yourself, or that you cheated by cleverly making it from three kitchen place mats, two napkin rings and a belt! Go ahead. Take all the credit!

Ingredients for this recipe

- 2 pieced and topstitched rectangular faux leather place mats for briefcase front and back
- Rectangular faux leather place mat with curved topstitching for flap
- Matching thread
- ¾" silver magnetic snap
- 1¼ yd. black boning (stays)
- Matching 1½" wide ladies belt for shoulder strap

- 3½ yd. of 1½" wide black grosgrain ribbon for gusset
- ¼ yd. single-sided fusible stabilizer, for gusset
- 2 thin silver napkin rings to attach gusset to shoulder strap
- Silver kitchen cabinet handle
- Matching silver cabinet back plate
- (2) 8-32 by ½" truss head or pan head machine bolts (slotted or Phillips head)
- Glue
- 4 pinch-type clothespins

Instructions

PREPARE THE PLACE MATS

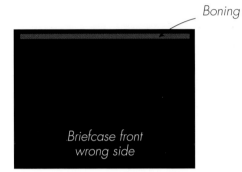

Boning

*Briefcase front
wrong side*

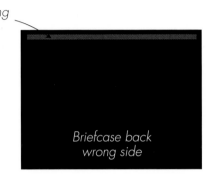

*Briefcase back
wrong side*

1 Prepare briefcase front and back place mats by topstitching the boning to the wrong side along top edges. This will stabilize and help the briefcase keep its shape when carried by the shoulder strap.

MAKE THE FLAP

3"

1 Center and pierce two holes in the flap place mat, 3" apart, as shown.

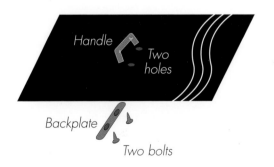

Handle

Two holes

Backplate

Two bolts

2 Securely screw handle to place mat with a screwdriver, placing the back plate on the wrong side. The back plate already has properly spaced holes in it. The back plate gives the top of the flap shape and keeps the screw heads from pulling through the place mat.

Do not iron vinyl or faux leather! You will melt it!

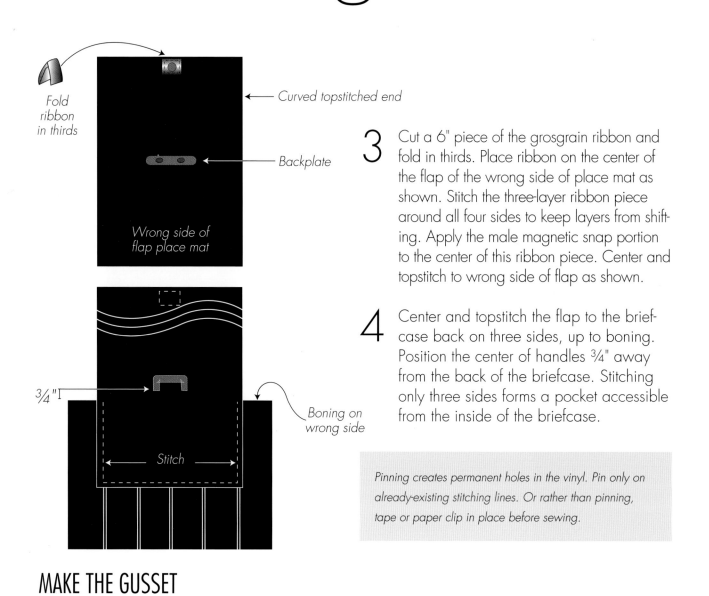

Fold ribbon in thirds

Curved topstitched end

Backplate

Wrong side of flap place mat

3 Cut a 6" piece of the grosgrain ribbon and fold in thirds. Place ribbon on the center of the flap of the wrong side of place mat as shown. Stitch the three-layer ribbon piece around all four sides to keep layers from shifting. Apply the male magnetic snap portion to the center of this ribbon piece. Center and topstitch to wrong side of flap as shown.

4 Center and topstitch the flap to the briefcase back on three sides, up to boning. Position the center of handles ¾" away from the back of the briefcase. Stitching only three sides forms a pocket accessible from the inside of the briefcase.

¾"

Boning on wrong side

Stitch

Pinning creates permanent holes in the vinyl. Pin only on already-existing stitching lines. Or rather than pinning, tape or paper clip in place before sewing.

MAKE THE GUSSET

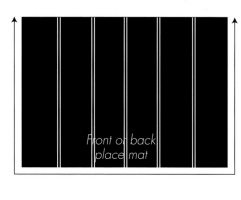

Front or back place mat

1 Measure around three sides of the front or back of the place mat and add 8" to this measurement. This is the length of the gusset. Cut a piece of fusible stabilizer the length of the gusset by 1¼" wide. (You will need to seam together to get a piece this long.) Cut a piece of grosgrain ribbon twice the length of the gusset plus 1".

2 Fold ribbon in half crosswise. Fold under cut ends ½". Center fusible stabilizer between ribbon layers and fuse in place. Topstitch ribbon edges together close to edge, without stitching through stabilizer.

Fold of ribbon

Ribbon

Timtex or Peltex

ASSEMBLE THE BRIEFCASE

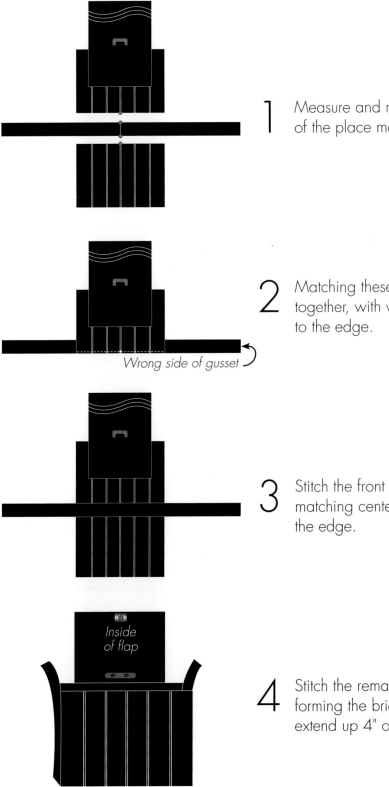

Wrong side of gusset

Inside of flap

1 Measure and mark the center of the front and back of the place mats and gusset.

2 Matching these center markings, join by topstitching together, with wrong sides together. Stitch very close to the edge.

3 Stitch the front of the briefcase in the same manner, matching center markings and stitching very close to the edge.

4 Stitch the remaining four sides in the same manner, forming the briefcase. The ends of the gusset will extend up 4" on each side.

ATTACH SHOULDER STRAP

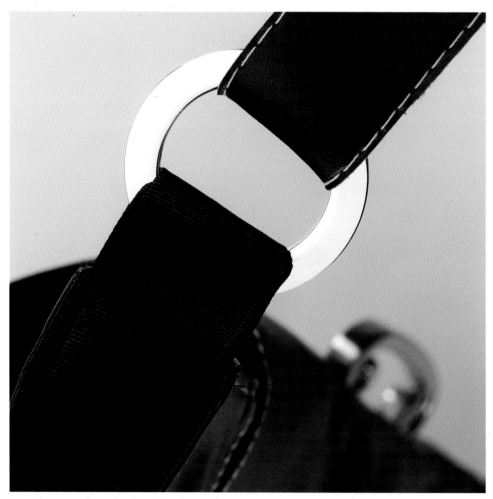

1 Loop napkin rings through the ends of the gusset. Fold the gusset ends to the inside 2" and stitch or glue and clamp securely in place.

2 Cut belt as shown.

3 Loop the belt ends through napkin rings. Fold the belt ends back 2" and stitch or glue and clamp securely in place. The length of the strap is adjustable with the belt buckle.

10"

Close up shot of side of briefcase showing where gusset and strap meet with ring.

ATTACH REMAINING SNAP

1 With the handle centered on the top of the briefcase, determine correct placement for remaining female portion of magnetic snap. Attach snap to front of briefcase, using a reinforcing square of fabric on the back.

GRAPE RUG TOTE WITH ZIPPER

Purple is my favorite color and it reminds me of the fertile grape-growing region an hour north of our Pennsylvania dairy farm. Miles of commercial vineyards fill the Lake Erie landscape with a fragrant aroma. In the Grape Rug Tote, two ample outside pockets close with hook-and-loop fastener, while the tote itself closes securely with a zipper.

Ingredients for this recipe

- 20" x 40" reversible fringed rug
- Matching reversible fringed place mat for pockets
- Matching thread
- 1½ yd. 1"-wide nylon or cotton webbing
- ¼ yd. coordinating fabric to cover webbing
- 4" of ¾"-wide hook-and-loop fastener
- Heavyweight zipper, minimum length 24"
- 4" of ¼" ribbon for zipper pull

Instructions

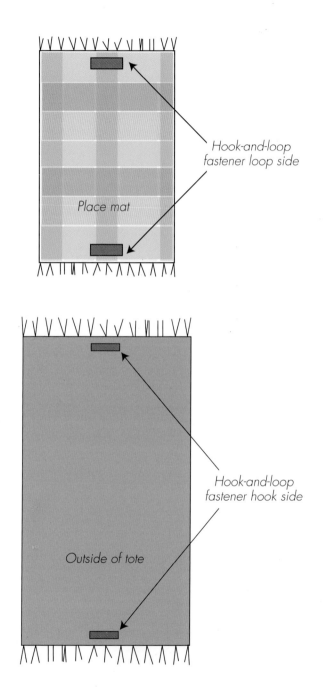

Hook-and-loop
fastener loop side

Place mat

Hook-and-loop
fastener hook side

Outside of tote

1 Cut hook-and-loop fastener in half. Center and topstitch the loop side of the hook-and-loop fastener to ends of place mat as shown.

2 Center and topstitch the hook side of the hook-and-loop fastener to ends of rug as shown.

Any seams too heavy to machine stitch can be glued with a bead of rubber cement glue and clamped with pinch-type clothespins or weighted with a pile of books until the glue is set.

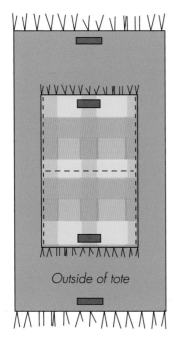

Outside of tote

3 Center place mat on rug and stitch sides and center partition to form two pockets as shown.

4 Fold rug ends down to meet the hook-and-loop closure on the place mat. Mark both resulting folds with pins.

5 To make two straps, cut webbing in half. If using nylon webbing, seal the cut ends with a candle or match so that they cannot fray. If using cotton webbing, zigzag ends so that they cannot fray.

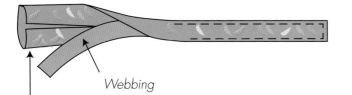

Webbing

4" strip, folded

6 Cut two strips of fabric 4" x 29". Fold and press fabric strip lengthwise so that both edges meet in the middle. Enclose webbing with fabric and stitch along all four edges as shown.

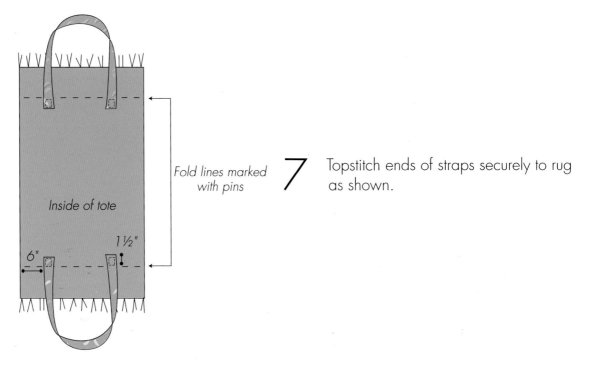

Fold lines marked with pins

Inside of tote

1 ½"

6"

7 Topstitch ends of straps securely to rug as shown.

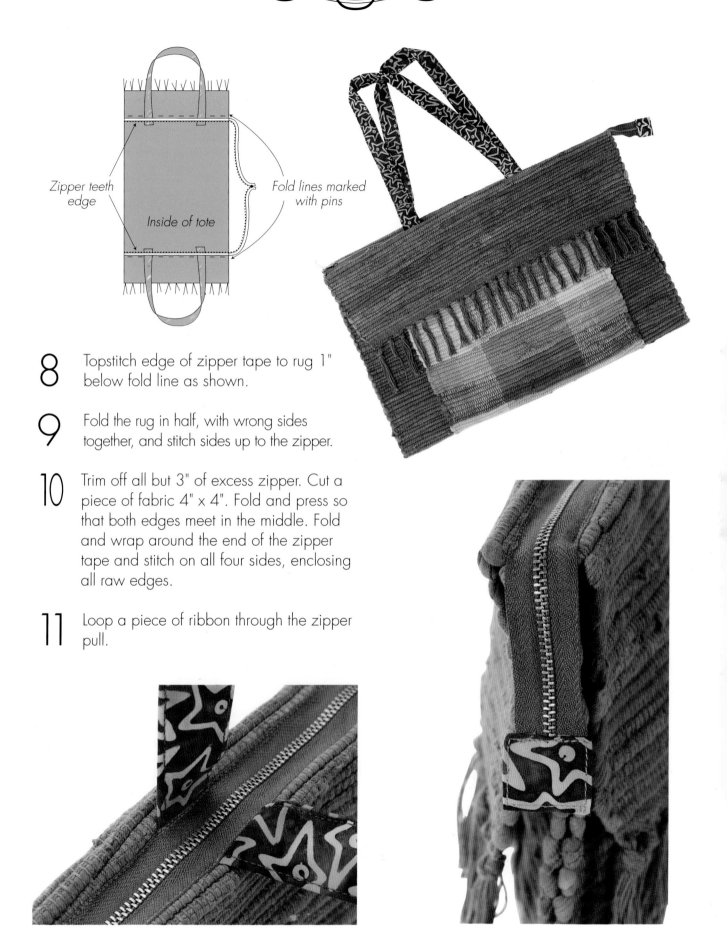

Zipper teeth edge

Fold lines marked with pins

Inside of tote

8 Topstitch edge of zipper tape to rug 1" below fold line as shown.

9 Fold the rug in half, with wrong sides together, and stitch sides up to the zipper.

10 Trim off all but 3" of excess zipper. Cut a piece of fabric 4" x 4". Fold and press so that both edges meet in the middle. Fold and wrap around the end of the zipper tape and stitch on all four sides, enclosing all raw edges.

11 Loop a piece of ribbon through the zipper pull.

BLUEBERRY RUG TOTE

Level of Difficulty

Four outside pockets keep you organized and on the go. This tote is named for the three lush blueberry bushes outside my back door. In the summer we must keep them covered with netting so we can eat more blueberries than the birds! We eat frozen blueberries for breakfast all winter stirred into homemade yogurt that I make from the milk from our dairy cows.

Ingredients for this recipe

- 20" x 40" reversible fringed rug
- Matching reversible fringed place mat for pockets
- Matching thread
- 1½ yd. of 1" wide nylon or cotton webbing
- 3" of ¾" wide hook-and-loop fastener

Instructions

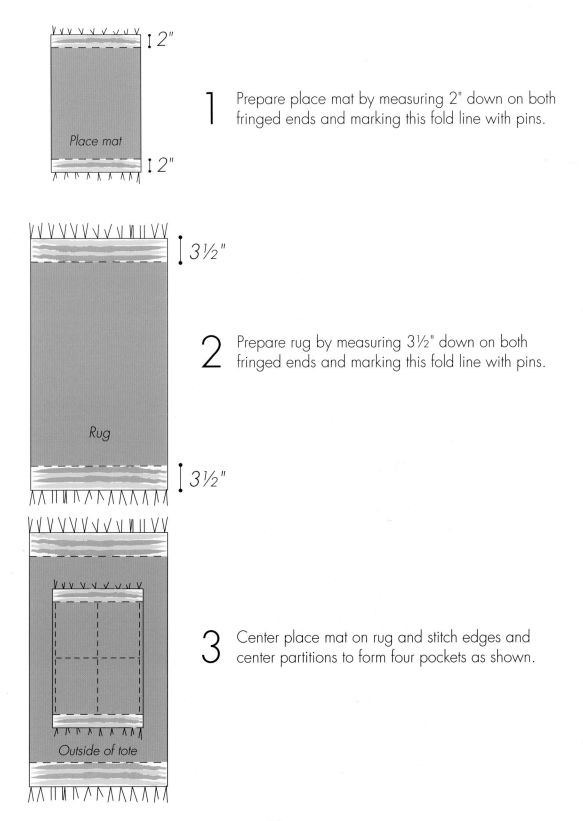

2"

Place mat

2"

1 Prepare place mat by measuring 2" down on both fringed ends and marking this fold line with pins.

3½"

Rug

3½"

2 Prepare rug by measuring 3½" down on both fringed ends and marking this fold line with pins.

Outside of tote

3 Center place mat on rug and stitch edges and center partitions to form four pockets as shown.

4 To make two straps, cut webbing in half. If using nylon webbing, seal the cut ends with a candle or match so that they cannot fray. If using cotton webbing, zigzag ends so that they cannot fray.

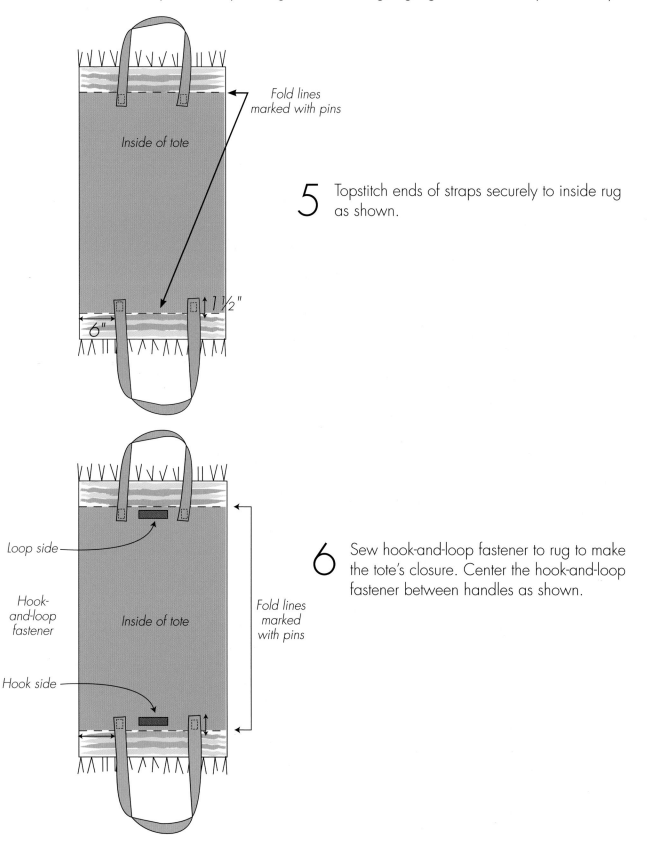

Fold lines marked with pins

Inside of tote

1 ½ "

6"

5 Topstitch ends of straps securely to inside rug as shown.

Loop side

Hook-and-loop fastener

Inside of tote

Fold lines marked with pins

Hook side

6 Sew hook-and-loop fastener to rug to make the tote's closure. Center the hook-and-loop fastener between handles as shown.

 Fold rug in half with wrong sides together and stitch sides up to the fold line.

8 Fold flaps down on fold lines and tack corners in place by handstitching.

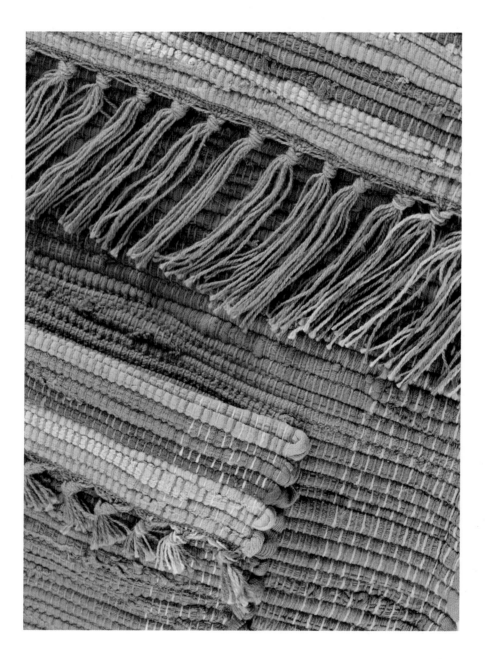

TUTTI FRUTTI RUG TOTE

Level of Difficulty

Try this recipe for a flavorful tote bag! Ingredients include a kitchen rug and two potholders. Tutti Frutti is multi colored to go with everything in your wardrobe. Two inside pockets made from potholders and a roomy interior provide space for any type of outing.

Ingredients for this recipe

- 27" x 45" reversible fringed rug
- 2 matching potholders for pockets
- Matching thread
- 1¾ yd. of 1½" - wide nylon or cotton webbing
- ½ yd. coordinating fabric to cover webbing
- 3" of ¾"- wide hook-and-loop fastener
- (2) ⅞" or 1" buttons

Instructions

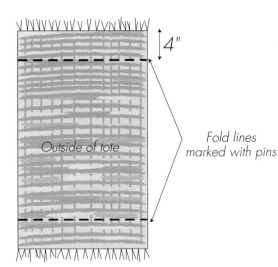

Outside of tote

4"

Fold lines
marked with pins

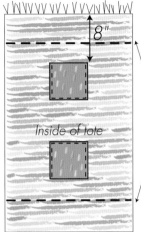

Inside of tote

8"

Fold lines marked
with pins

1 Prepare rug by measuring 4" down on both fringed ends and marking this fold line with pins.

2 Topstitch sides and bottom of two potholders to rug to form two inside pockets as shown.

3 To make two straps, cut webbing in half. If using nylon webbing, seal the cut ends with a candle or match so that they cannot fray. If using cotton webbing, zigzag ends so that they cannot fray.

4 Cut two strips of fabric 6" x 33". Fold and press fabric strip lengthwise so that both edges meet in the middle. Enclose webbing with fabric and stitch along all four edges as shown.

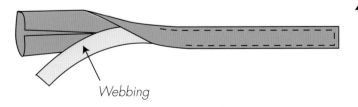

Webbing

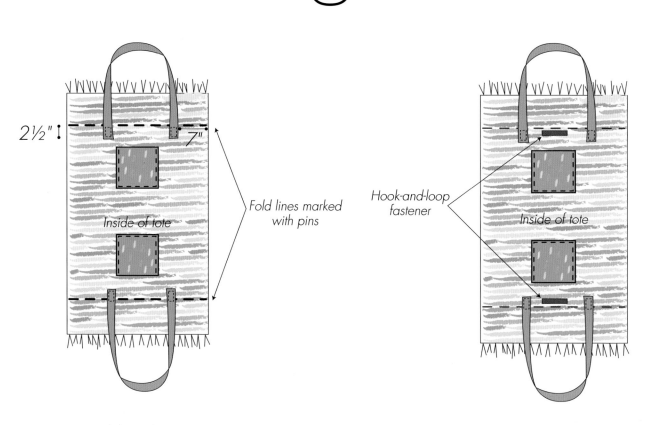

2½" ↕   7″

Inside of tote

Fold lines marked
with pins

Hook-and-loop
fastener

Inside of tote

5 Topstitch ends of straps securely to rug as shown.

6 Sew hook-and-loop fastener to rug to make the tote's closure. Center the hook-and-loop fastener between handles as shown.

Multiple-stitch
zigzag

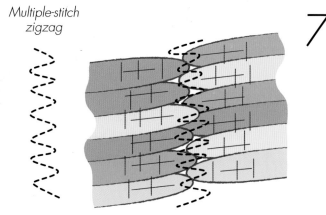

7 Fold rug in half, butting side edges tightly together. With the widest multiple-stitch zigzag (this stitch has individual stitches in each zig and zag, giving it more strength) stitch sides up to the fringed edge. It is all right if you cannot get all the way into the bottom corner. Stop machine stitching an inch or two away from the corner and whip stitch by hand.

Customize your rug tote with inside pockets to suit your individual needs.

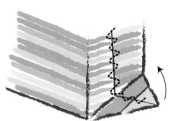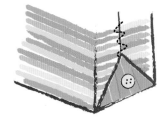

8 Box both bottom corners as shown and tack up with buttons.

9 Fold top cuff down on fold line.

These "rugged" totes are washable and will wear like iron. Take full advantage of the rug's fringed ends and finished edges. Casual, sensible and practical; these totes can "step" into the role of diaper bag, camera bag, overnighter, quilt class tote, gym bag, beach bag, airline carry-on, or briefcase. So "Step on it!" and make one soon! (Just make sure you don't choose a rug so large that your tote needs its own zip code!)

ASIAN-INSPIRED BACKPACK

Who would guess that this stylish backpack is a place mat makeover? Drawing its inspiration from the far-away Orient, this backpack lends a mysterious and exotic flair to an otherwise unglamorous outing. You deserve a touch of drama and adventure!

Ingredients for this recipe

- 2 rectangular satin or Asian print place mats*
- ¼ yd. coordinating fabric for flap
- ½ yd. heavy weight fusible interfacing
- Matching thread
- 2 belts with buckles (Use girls' belts for backpack sizes small and medium; women's belts for backpack sizes large and extra large.)
- ¾" magnetic snap
- 8 metal ¼" eyelets
- 1 yd. drawstring (a strong cord or ribbon that will slide through the eyelets easily)
- Cord lock
- 2 foreign coins with holes in the middle for cord ends
- Glue
- 4 pinch-type clothespins
- 3" tassel for embellishment
- Optional: 6" square of fabric for inside pocket
- * Place mats used in this project were purchased at Pier 1 Imports.

The best tassels are found in the Home Decorating Department of the fabric store.

Instructions

PREPARE THE PLACE MATS

1 Fold down the finished top edge of two of the place mats 1¼" to the inside and stitch.

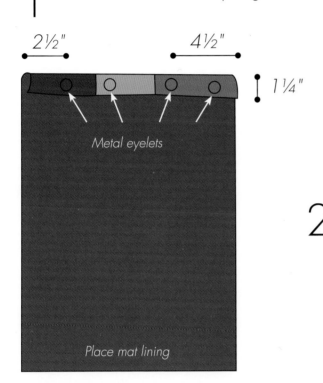

2½"   4½"

1¼"

Metal eyelets

Place mat lining

2 Apply metal eyelets to both place mats according to manufacturer's directions where shown.

MAKE THE FLAP WITH MAGNETIC SNAP CLOSURE

1 Cut two flaps from coordinating satin fabric using the pattern from page 74.

2 Interface both silk flaps with heavy fusible interfacing following manufacturer's directions.

3 Apply male half of magnetic snap to under-flap where shown on pattern, using a reinforcing square of heavy fabric on the back.

4 Stitch flaps, right sides together, along curved edges, pivoting at points and leaving top straight edge open.

5 Clip curves, trim corners, turn right side out and press.

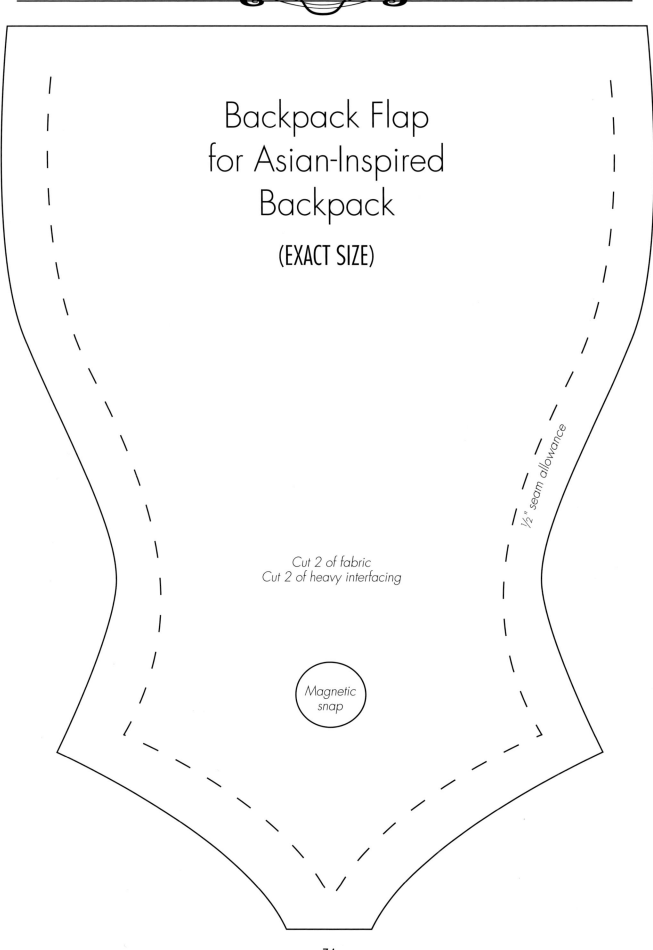

Backpack Flap
for Asian-Inspired
Backpack

(EXACT SIZE)

Cut 2 of fabric
Cut 2 of heavy interfacing

½" seam allowance

Magnetic snap

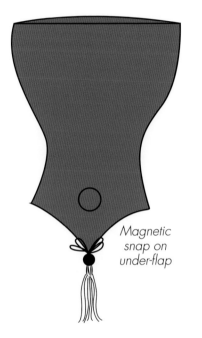

*Magnetic
snap on
under-flap*

6 Topstitch curved edges.

7 Serge or zigzag top raw edges together.

8 Handstitch tassel to point. Set flap aside.

ADD THE POCKETS

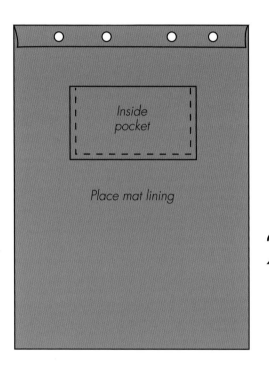

Inside pocket

Place mat lining

1 To create an inside pocket, turn under ¼" on all four sides of the 6" x 6" fabric. Turn under 1" hem along top edge and stitch.

2 Topstitch sides and bottom of pocket to inside of place mat.

The American Chiropractic Association says a backpack shouldn't hang more than 4" below your waist.

ASSEMBLE BACKPACK

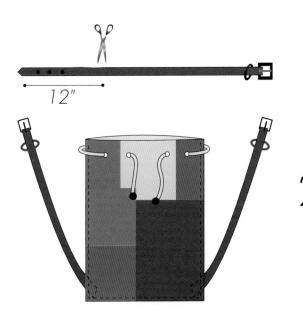

1 Cut both belts as shown.

2 Topstitch front place mat to back place mat, with wrong sides together along sides and bottom, inserting ends of belt. If the belts are too heavy to stitch through, glue this area and clamp with clothespins until glue is set.

3 Pull drawstring through eyelets and slide the cord lock over both ends together. Loop drawstring ends through coins, fold back and hand-stitch to make stoppers so the cord lock can't slide off.

Back of belts

Back of backpack

4 Place remaining belt ends inside backpack back at top as shown. Stitch or glue and clamp in place.

5 Apply flap to inside of backpack, covering the belt ends and topstitch in place.

6 Apply remaining female half of magnetic snap to backpack front, using a reinforcing square of fabric on the back.

FAUX LEATHER BACKPACK

Level of Difficulty

Throw on this practical backpack for hands-free shopping. Sensible pockets inside and out keep you organized and on the move. Add more pockets to personalize and customize to your individual needs.

Ingredients for this recipe

- 3 rectangular faux leather or faux suede place mats
- Matching thread
- 2 belts with buckles (Use girls' belts for backpack sizes small and medium; women's belts for backpack sizes large and extra large.)
- ¾" magnetic snap
- 8 metal ¼" eyelets
- 1 yd. drawstring (a strong cord or ribbon that will slide through the eyelets easily)
- 2 wooden pony beads for cord ends
- Glue
- 4 pinch-type clothespins
- Optional: 6" square of fabric for inside pocket

Instructions

PREPARE THE PLACE MATS

1   Fold down the finished top edge of two of the place mats 1 ¼" to the inside and stitch.

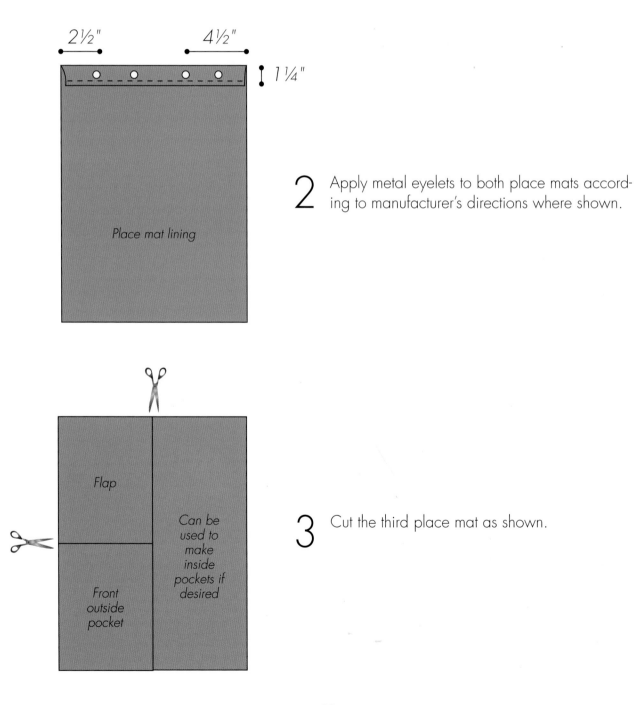

2   Apply metal eyelets to both place mats according to manufacturer's directions where shown.

3   Cut the third place mat as shown.

ADD THE POCKETS

1 Turn under both cut edges of front pocket ¼" and stitch.

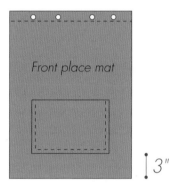

Front place mat

3"

2 Topstitch sides and bottom of pocket to front place mat, 3" up from edge.

3 To create an inside pocket, turn under ¼" on all four sides of the 6" x 6" fabric. Turn under 1" hem along top edge and stitch.

Inside pocket

Place mat lining

4 Topstitch sides and bottom of pocket to inside of place mat.

MAKE THE FLAP WITH MAGNETIC SNAP CLOSURE

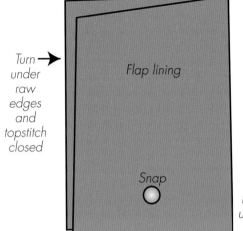

Turn under raw edges and topstitch closed →

Flap lining

Snap

Place snap 1" up from bottom of flap

1 If the place mat has a separate lining on the back: Fold seam allowances back along side of flap and pin in place. Apply male half of magnetic snap to lining only, centering from side to side. Use a reinforcing square of heavy fabric on the back if necessary. Topstitch side of the flap closed.

If the place mat does not have a separate lining on the back, but is all one layer: Apply snap. Cut a piece of fabric 1" larger than flap on all sides. Turn edges under and topstitch to back of flap to hide the snap prongs and washer. Set flap aside.

ASSEMBLE BACKPACK

12"

1 Cut belts as shown.

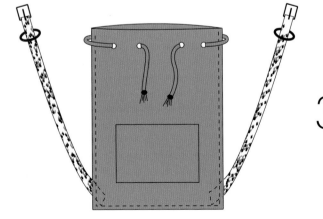

2 With wrong sides together topstitch front place mat to back place mat, inserting ends of belt along sides and bottom. If the belts are too heavy to stitch through, glue this area and clamp with clothespins until glue is set.

3 Pull drawstring through eyelets and glue beads to ends.

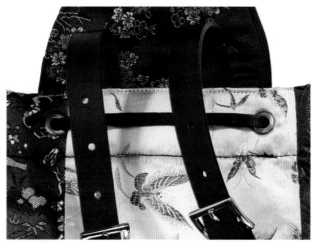

Attach belt ends and flap to backpack as in the Asian-Inspired Backpack.

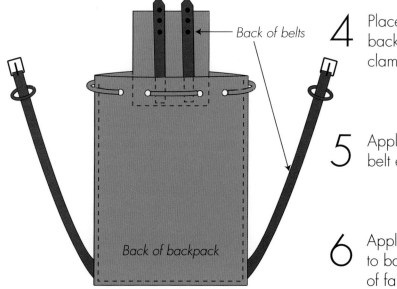

Back of belts

Back of backpack

4 Place remaining belt ends inside backpack back at top as shown. Stitch or glue and clamp in place.

5 Apply flap to inside of backpack, covering the belt ends and topstitch in place.

6 Apply remaining female half of magnetic snap to backpack front, using a reinforcing square of fabric on the back.

Paducah, KY, is highly regarded as "Quilt City, USA." This city, with a population of 27,000, plays host to an additional 40,000 quilters and visitors during the annual American Quilters Society Quilt Show. One year while in Paducah to teach and vend, we overheard a teenage boy ask the clerk at a convenience store, "What is going on? Is there a Grandma Convention in town?"

CHAPTER 5

A WINTER ENSEMBLE

Get out of the kitchen, but take your potholders, oven mitts and these gourmet recipes with you! These luxurious fur-trimmed fashion accessories will transform you from a potholder-dependent domestic into a sophisticated socialite!

Cheryl's Tips for Working with Furs:

Faux furs and genuine furs use the same techniques. Furs have a nap, just like corduroy and velvet. Make sure you cut all pieces going the same direction. Cut out pieces individually because they will slide too much if cut together in layers. For accuracy, trace the cutting line on the back of the hide or fabric backing with a marker. Then, cut with the very tips of the scissors, sliding the tips to cut only the hide or backing fabric, not the hairs. Hairs will separate as you pull apart. Never use a rotary cutter. Shake the pieces outside or your sewing room will look like you have a house pet that sheds! A leather machine needle is needed for genuine furs. It is triangular in shape and sharp on the three edges, cutting a hole in the hide for each stitch. Faux furs can be stitched with a sharp- or universal-point machine needle. Use a narrow seam allowance to reduce bulk. When sewing, push the hairs out of the way of the seam allowance, toward the body of the project, catching as few as possible in the seam. If many hairs are caught in the seam when you look at it from the right side, pick them out with a seam ripper or brush the seam with a toothbrush to pull them out. Never press or steam fur! Finger press to crease and shape. Send to a reputable dry cleaner when soiled.

QUILTED SHOULDER PURSE

Level of Difficulty

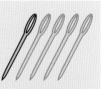

This is a small purse with a big attitude! Swing it flirtatiously from your shoulder or shorten the chain handle by doubling it back and hooking both hooks on the same loop.

Ingredients for this recipe

- 2 white quilted potholders with hanging loops
- 3 black fur pompons with twill tape (or ribbon) for attaching
- 3" x 20" piece black fur
- 2½" x 20" black lining fabric
- Matching thread
- ¾" silver magnetic snap
- 42" black nickel shoulder chain with hooks or clips on ends

Note: All potholders and oven mitts used in this chapter were purchased at Ikea.

Instructions

1 Lay out potholders with both hanging loops in upper left corners. The hanging loops will be used to attach the shoulder chain. Pin pompons by the twill tape to the bottom of one potholder, evenly spaced apart.

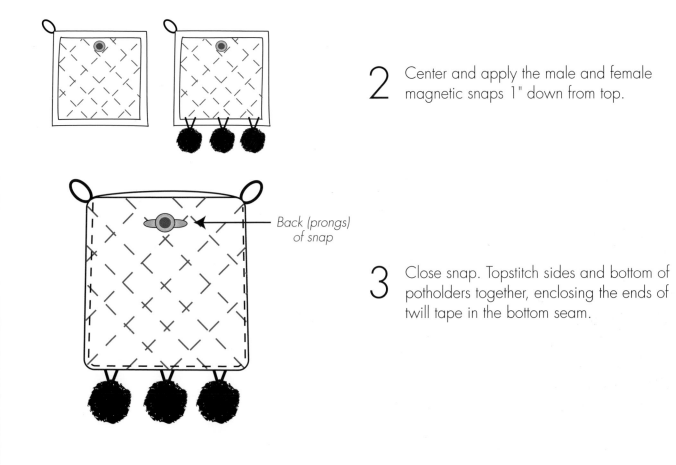

2 Center and apply the male and female magnetic snaps 1" down from top.

Back (prongs) of snap

3 Close snap. Topstitch sides and bottom of potholders together, enclosing the ends of twill tape in the bottom seam.

4 Measure both the fur and lining strips to fit around the top of the purse plus 2".

If you cannot find individual fur pompons, look for fur pompon trim by the yard and clip them off the header tape. Our fur yardage (for the cuffs) was recycled from a never-to-be-worn-again fur coat. There is enough left to add a fur collar and cuffs to a wool or denim coat to make a picture perfect winter ensemble! Genuine fur and faux fur work equally as well for these projects.

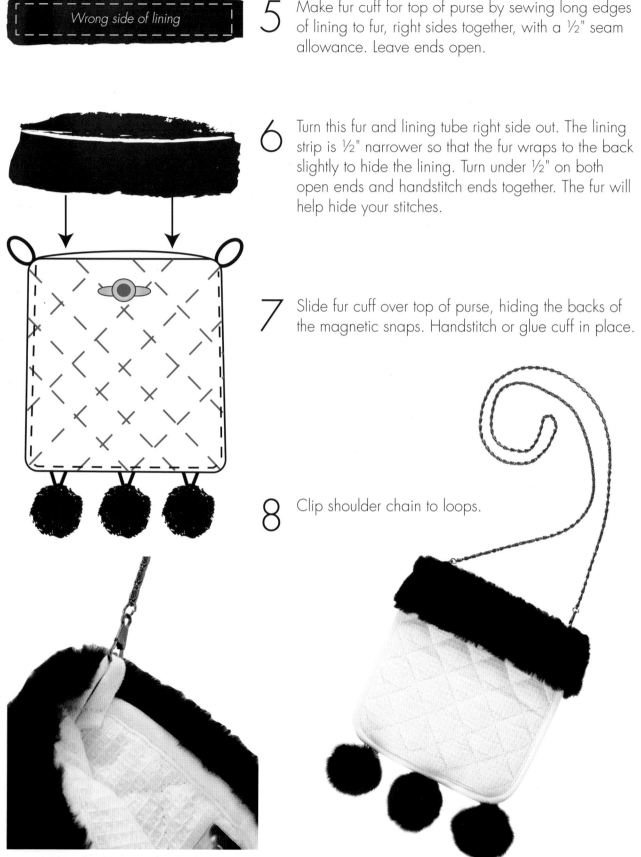

Wrong side of lining

5 Make fur cuff for top of purse by sewing long edges of lining to fur, right sides together, with a ½" seam allowance. Leave ends open.

6 Turn this fur and lining tube right side out. The lining strip is ½" narrower so that the fur wraps to the back slightly to hide the lining. Turn under ½" on both open ends and handstitch ends together. The fur will help hide your stitches.

7 Slide fur cuff over top of purse, hiding the backs of the magnetic snaps. Handstitch or glue cuff in place.

8 Clip shoulder chain to loops.

Chain hooked to potholder loop.

QUILTED HAT

Level of Difficulty

Framing your face in plush fur, this warm hat not only looks great, but really chases away the winter chills. The satin lining promises to not mess up your hair.

Ingredients for this recipe

- 6 white quilted potholders, at least 8" square
- ¼ yd. white satin lining fabric
- 3½" x 25½" piece black fur
- 3" x 25½" black lining fabric
- Matching thread

Instructions

1 Using the hat pattern, cut a hat piece from each of the six potholders. Using the same hat pattern, cut six white lining pieces.

2 Join quilted hat pieces together in two sets of three, right sides together, using a ¼" seam allowance. Join both sets of three together with one continuous seam, using a ¼" seam allowance.

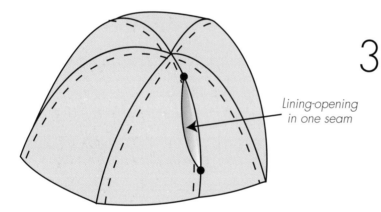

Lining-opening in one seam

3 Join hat lining pieces together in two sets of three, right sides together, using a ¼" seam allowance. On one of these seams, leave a 5" opening for turning. Join both sets of three together with one continuous seam, using a ¼" seam allowance. Set lining aside.

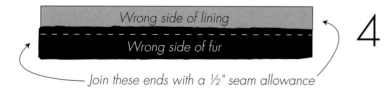

Wrong side of lining

Wrong side of fur

Join these ends with a ½" seam allowance

4 Make fur cuff for hat by sewing black lining to fur along one long edge, right sides together, with a ½" seam allowance. Open and stitch ends, right sides together, with a ½" seam allowance, making a circle. Fold cuff in half, wrong sides together, matching raw edges.

This is a one-size-fits-all hat pattern, but try it on a couple times throughout the construction to see if you need to make any size adjustments.

Hat Pattern
(EXACT SIZE)

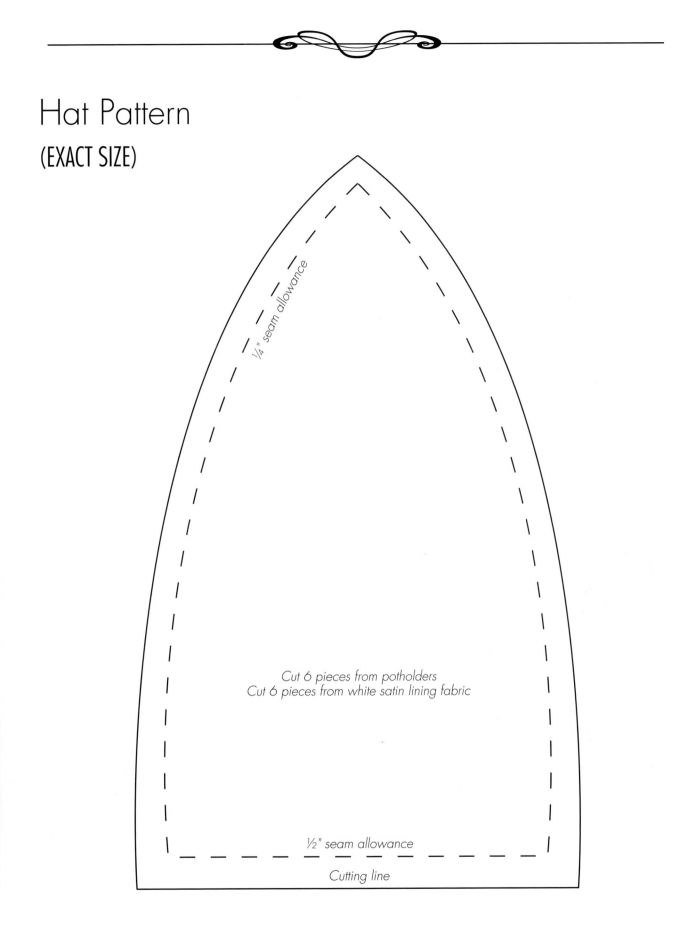

¼" seam allowance

Cut 6 pieces from potholders
Cut 6 pieces from white satin lining fabric

½" seam allowance

Cutting line

5 Pin then stitch fur cuff to quilted hat, lining side of cuff and right side of hat together, with a ½" seam allowance.

Fur

6 Pin then stitch lining to hat, right sides together, stitching over previous stitching.

7 Turn hat right-side out through opening in lining. Handstitch lining opening closed.

Lining

8 Shape hat by pulling cuff down and making sure the lining and all seam allowances are up inside the hat. Pin. Topstitch these layers in place as shown. The free arm of your sewing machine is a great help for this step. Hand tack lining to hat at crown. Fold cuff back and admire yourself in the mirror with your new hat on!

QUILTED SCARF

Face the chilly weather in style. Laugh at the cold as you toss this cozy scarf across your shoulder!

Ingredients for this recipe

- 6 white quilted potholders
- 3 yd. white ¼" or ½" double fold bias tape
- 6 black fur pompons with twill tape (or ribbon) for attaching
- (2) 3" x 14" pieces black fur
- (2) 2½" x 14" black lining fabric
- Matching thread

If you want a longer scarf, simply use more potholders!

Instructions

1 Butt potholders together end to end. Join with the widest multiple-stitch zigzag (this stitch has individual stitches in each zig and zag, giving it more strength).

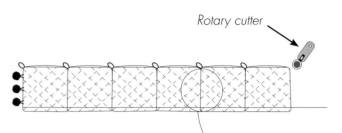

Rotary cutter

2 Lay a ruler along the sides of the potholder strip. Using a rotary cutter, trim off sides to make a quilted strip 6" wide.

3 Finish these long cut edges with double fold bias tape.

Close up of multiple-stitch zig zag

4 Sew three pompons by the twill tape to both ends, evenly spaced.

5 Make two fur cuffs for the ends of the scarf as you did in steps 5 and 6 for the purse on page 88.

6 Slide fur cuffs over ends of scarf, hiding where the pompons are sewn. Handstitch or glue cuffs in place.

QUILTED MITTENS

Level of Difficulty

It is hard to believe that these posh fur-trimmed fashion accessories were unassuming oven mitts in their first life! Pamper your friends and make some as gifts.

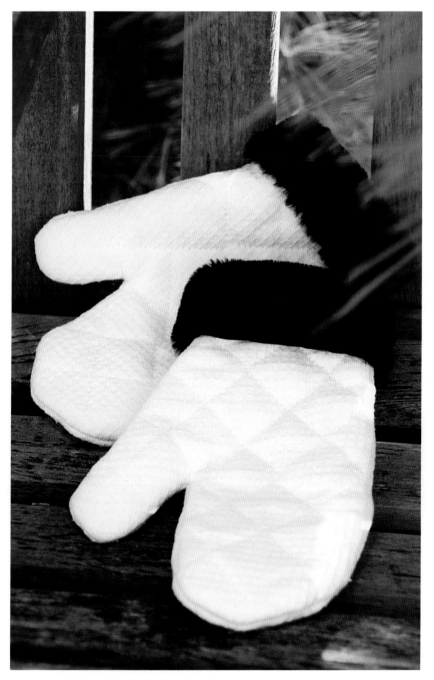

Ingredients for this recipe

- 2 white quilted oven mitts
- (2) 3" x 10½" piece black fur
- (2) 2½" x 10½" black lining fabric
- Matching thread

Instructions

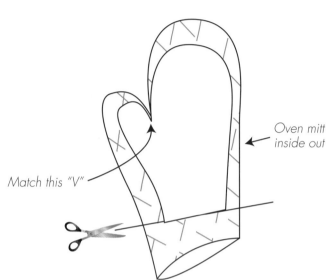

Match this "V"

Oven mitt inside out

1 Turn both oven mitts inside out. Pin mitten pattern to oven mitts, matching the stitching at the "V" where the thumb meets the hand. Trace outline of mitten pattern to wrong sides of oven mitts. These are your new stitching lines to make the mitts smaller.

2 Cut off excess from bottom of oven mitts. Serge or zigzag these raw edges.

3 Stitch along traced stitching lines. At the "V," stitch over the manufacturer's original stitching line. Trim seam allowances to ¼". Serge or zigzag the seam allowances together.

4 Turn both mittens right side out. Make two fur cuffs as you did in step 4 for the hat on page 90.

5 Pin, then stitch fur cuffs to mittens, wrong sides together. Stitch with a ½" seam allowance. The free arm of your sewing machine is a great help for this. Fold and tack cuffs to the right side.

Quilted Mittens
Pattern
(EXACT SIZE)

CHAPTER 6
WEEKENDER TRAVEL COLLECTION

Take it from someone who knows, this is everything you need to keep organized and on track during your next business trip or fun get-away. My career as a speaker, teacher and designer means I spend a great deal of time away from home in hotel rooms. Whether traveling by car or plane, organization is the key to a successful trip and these handsome accessories help you arrive organized and in style.

LUGGAGE TAG

Level of Difficulty

This luggage tag's jumbo size and bright colors will help you spot your suitcase on the carousel in baggage claim. Always put your contact information inside your suitcase as well, just in case the luggage tag comes up missing.

Ingredients for this recipe

- Quilted potholder or 6½" x 3½" piece of quilted fabric
- 2 pieces of 8 gauge clear vinyl 7" x 4"
- Business card or heavy paper printed with your contact information
- ¼" metal eyelet
- ½ yd. ⅜" wide ribbon or cord
- Matching thread

Pattern Piece

(ACTUAL SIZE)

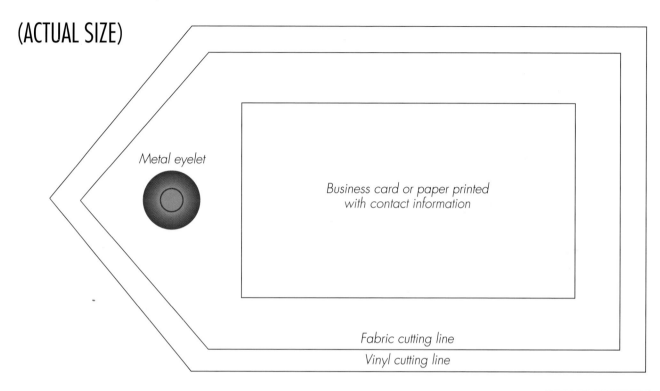

Metal eyelet

Business card or paper printed with contact information

Fabric cutting line

Vinyl cutting line

Instructions

1 Cut one piece of quilted fabric following the fabric cutting line on pattern. Cut two pieces of clear vinyl following the vinyl cutting line on the pattern.

2 Center and layer as shown. Topstitch around business card and through vinyl around fabric edge.

3 Apply metal eyelet to tag according to manufacturer's directions. Thread the ribbon or cord through eyelet and tie securely to suitcase.

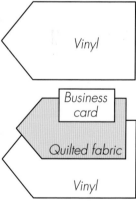

Vinyl

Business card

Quilted fabric

Vinyl

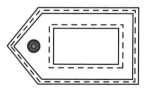

Avoid pinning clear vinyl because it leaves permanent holes. Try paper clips or tape instead. If the vinyl grips the presser foot or throat plate as you stitch, preventing it from feeding evenly, cover with one ply of a tissue then stitch. Tissue is transparent enough to see or feel through and you can tear it away later. And of course never iron vinyl!

EYEGLASS HOLDER

Level of Difficulty

This is not only the perfect size for eyeglasses, but also your cell phone, digital camera, iPod or MP3 Player. Use the loop to hook it to your purse or belt. Quilters love this little case to transport their rotary cutter to class. This little project is easy enough to teach a child to sew. Tell her it is a sleeping bag for one of her little dolls!

Ingredients for this recipe

- 7" or 8" square quilted potholder
- ⅝" button
- Matching thread

Instructions

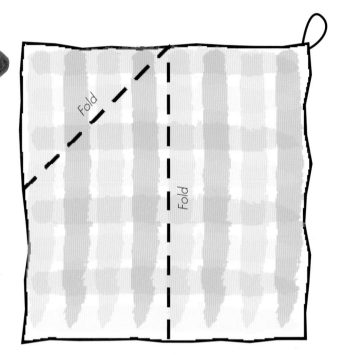

1   Fold potholder in half. Stitch bottom and side below flap.

2   Fold down flap and tack flap down with a button.

SLEEP EYE MASK

Level of Difficulty

Living in the country, I am not used to street lights or traffic at night. Even the light coming in under the hotel room door is enough to keep me awake. This little sleep mask has become a treasured traveling companion, along with my earplugs to block out the sounds of trains, planes and the party next door. Must get my beauty sleep!

Ingredients for this recipe

- Quilted potholder, minimum length 8" or piece of soft quilted fabric 8" x 4"
- 24" of ¼" or ½" coordinating double fold bias tape
- 15" of ¼" or ⅜" wide elastic for strap
- Matching thread

Mask Piece

(ACTUAL SIZE)

Instructions

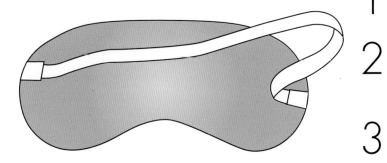

1 Cut a piece of quilted fabric according to the pattern.

2 Pin ends of elastic to mask as shown. Try on mask to test for comfortable fit and adjust elastic as necessary.

3 Finish edges with double fold bias tape following manufacturer's directions, enclosing ends of elastic.

Put one of these sleep masks, earplugs, tissues and some potpourri on the night stand in your guest room. Make your eye mask from two fabric layers and fill with a couple spoonfuls of dried lavender or flax seed before binding for a relaxing scent. These little frivolous touches make your guests feel welcome and pampered!

If I have a mini-fridge in my hotel room, I keep my eye mask there till needed. It soothes my puffy bloodshot eyes after a long day!

HEATPROOF CURLING IRON CADDY

Your hair is the last thing you do before you run out the door! How many times have you waved your curling iron around trying to cool it off to pack it in your suitcase?

Ingredients for this recipe

- Quilted oven mitt
- Matching thread

Instructions

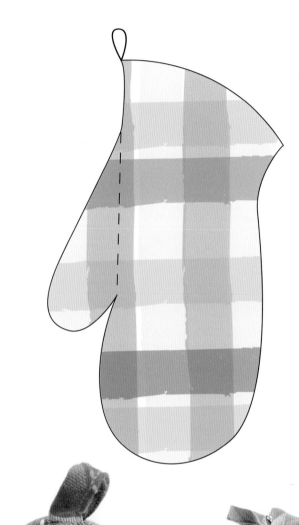

1   Turn oven mitt inside out. Draw a line as shown from the "V" where the thumb meets the hand to the mitt opening.

2   Stitch along drawn line. Trim seam allowance to ¼". Serge or zigzag the seam allowances together.

3   Turn mitt right side out. The loop can be used for hanging the caddy in the bathroom. There is enough room to slide your comb and brush inside, too.

SHOE BAG

Level of Difficulty

Sand from the beach? Mud from a rainy day? Whatever has made your shoes a mess, keep them isolated from the rest of your suitcase with this shoe bag.

Ingredients for this recipe

- Rectangular place mat
- 22" zipper
- 4" of ¼" ribbon for zipper pull
- Matching thread

Instructions

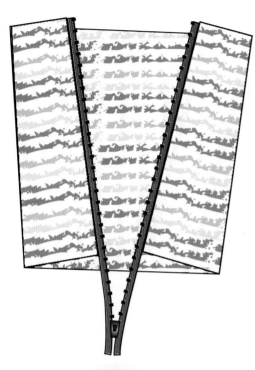

1 Topstitch zipper to ends of place mat as shown.

2 Close zipper. Fold place mat so that zipper is centered on the front of the shoe bag. Tuck in end of zipper to form a hanging loop.

3 Topstitch ends of bag closed.

4 Loop a piece of ribbon through the zipper pull.

Caught in the rain? Need to bring home a wet garment or swimsuit? There is a plastic bag in your hotel room ice bucket, a larger one in the bottom of your wastebasket, and a plastic laundry bag in your closet. Even the complimentary plastic shower cap can be used to isolate small items.

COSMETIC BAG

Level of Difficulty

This quilted super-size cosmetic bag is large enough to carry all your beauty must-haves.

Ingredients for this recipe

- Oval quilted place mat
- 22" zipper
- Matching thread
- 4" of ¼" ribbon for zipper pull

Instructions

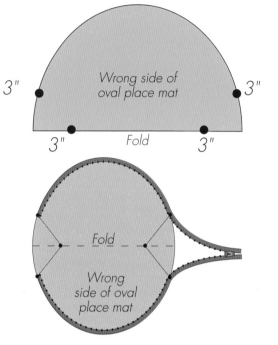

1 Fold place mat in half. Measure in from fold 3" and up from fold 3". Connect these points with a fabric marking pen on the wrong side of the place mat. These lines will be your stitching lines.

2 Open zipper and topstitch zipper to place mat between markings as shown.

3 Close zipper most of the way with right sides of place mat together.

4 Stitch on marked stitching lines, stitching through zipper tapes. Trim off excess end of zipper. Open zipper and turn cosmetic bag right side out.

5 Loop a piece of ribbon through the zipper pull.

Nicki, my booth helper, and I were in a noisy restaurant in Atlanta after a busy show day. I turned in time to hear a 20-something young man ask Nicki, "So, where do you hang this roll-up art? Is it like a window shade?"

Nicki raised her voice again and answered, "I said we design wearable art, not roll-up art!"

PLACE MAT PURSE

Level of Difficulty

Once you arrive at your destination, you will of course need a matching purse for sightseeing, shopping or meetings.

Ingredients for this recipe

- Rectangular place mat
- Matching tea towel, cloth napkin or ¼ yd. coordinating fabric for rod pockets
- Coordinating potholder for pocket
- Matching thread
- Bamboo purse handles with removable rods

Instructions

1 Fold place mat in half and mark fold with pins.

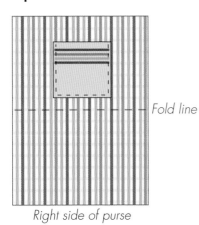

Fold line

Right side of purse

2 Center potholder on one half and stitch three sides to form pocket on outside of purse.

3 To make the rod pockets for the handles, cut two pieces of fabric each measuring 7¼" x 3".

4 Serge or zigzag raw edges. Press under short ends ½" and topstitch.

5 Fold both rod pocket strips in half length-wise, wrong sides together, and stitch long edges together with a ½" seam allowance.

Wrong side of purse

6 Center and topstitch rod pocket strips to wrong side of purse so that rod pockets extend above the top of the purse.

7 Fold up and topstitch sides together.

8 Attach handle by inserting rods through the rod pockets and securing nuts.

These bamboo handles are detachable, so make several interchangeable fabric bags and switch the same handles back and forth for endless combinations.

SNUG AS A RUG CARRY-ALL

Level of Difficulty

I carry this bag as my "purse" when flying. My boarding passes, itinerary and cell phone are all within easy reach in the front pockets. My regular purse, snacks and reading material drop inside. (Create an optional hidden zippered security pocket inside for extra money and your passport.) I can carry it over my shoulder or loop it over the handle of my wheeled carry-on suitcase. I even folded it in half and used it as a pillow for a nap on the plane.

Ingredients for this recipe

- 20" x 30" striped woven rug*
- Matching potholder for pocket*
- Matching striped tea towel or ½ yd. coordinating fabric to cover webbing and for inside pockets*

- 1½ yd. of 1" wide nylon or cotton webbing
- Matching thread
- * Items used in this project were purchased at Bed, Bath and Beyond.

Instructions

1 Fold the rug in half and mark fold with pins.

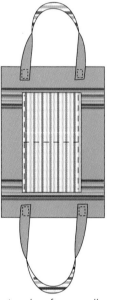

Fold line

Outside of bag

2 Center potholder on one half and stitch three sides to form pocket on the outside of the bag.

3 To make two straps, cut webbing in half. If using nylon webbing, seal the cut ends with a candle or match so that they cannot fray. If using cotton webbing, zigzag ends so that they cannot fray.

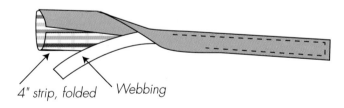

4" strip, folded   *Webbing*

4 Cut two strips of fabric 4" x 29" long. Fold and press each fabric strip lengthwise so that both edges meet in the middle. Enclose webbing with fabric and stitch along all four edges as shown.

5 Topstitch ends of straps securely to outside of rug as shown.

Inside of carry-all

6 Use remaining fabric from covering the straps to make inside pockets. To make pockets, cut a piece of fabric 10" x 25". (Slightly smaller or larger will work, it depends on how much fabric you have left over from the straps.) Serge or zigzag raw edges and turn under ½" and stitch. Center on inside of bag and stitch sides and center partition to form two pockets as shown.

7 Fold rug in half, with wrong sides together, and stitch sides.

Look for a pocket-type potholder that has a place to slide your hand into when handling hot dishes. (It works like an oven mitt without a thumb.) This provides you with two pockets in one.

GARMENT BAG

Level of Difficulty

This garment bag will serve you well for a driving trip. Hang it in the back seat or lay it across the top of your suitcases. It is not recommended for checked airline luggage.

Ingredients for this recipe

- 52" x 52" rectangular tablecloth
- 3" x 4½" piece clear vinyl for business card pocket
- Business card or heavy paper printed with your contact information
- 36" or 45" zipper for front of garment bag
- 4" of ¼" ribbon for zipper pull

- 2 coordinating potholders for front pockets
- (2) 8" zippers for front pockets (we used novelty zippers with pull rings)
- Coordinating rectangular place mat for shoe pocket on back
- Matching thread
- Sturdy wooden hanger

Instructions

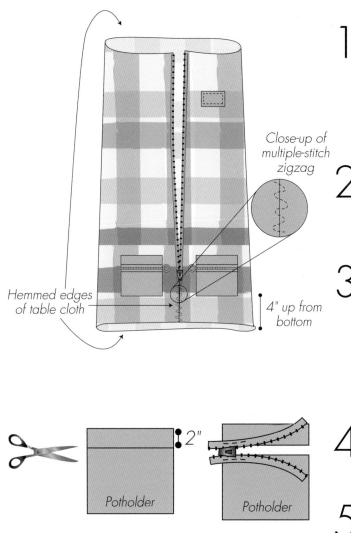

Close-up of multiple-stitch zigzag

Hemmed edges of table cloth

4" up from bottom

2"

Potholder

Potholder

1 With zipper open, pin top of zipper tape ½" down from top. Topstitch zipper over hemmed edges of tablecloth. Close seam below zipper by butting tablecloth hemmed edges together and stitching with a wide multiple-stitch zigzag.

2 Loop a piece of ribbon through the zipper pull. Close zipper. Fold tablecloth so that zipper is centered on the front of the garment bag. Mark side folds with pins.

3 To make both lower outside zippered pockets, cut potholders as shown. Serge or zigzag raw edges. Spread edges ½" apart and topstitch zipper to edges, turning ends of zipper tape to the back. Make sure one pocket opens from the left and one from the right.

4 Center and topstitch pockets to lower front of bag, 4" up from bottom.

5 Topstitch three sides of vinyl to upper right side to form an ID pocket. Insert business card or paper printed with contact information.

If your garments arrive a bit wrinkled, hang them on the back of the bathroom door while you shower to steam out the wrinkles. Need to hand launder a garment in the hotel room? Shampoo makes a great laundry detergent substitute in a pinch. After all, it is formulated to remove body oils and perspiration from natural fibers. Hair conditioner can replace fabric softener. It leaves a pleasant scent and stops static cling as well. Your hair dryer can speed up drying. If there is no hair dryer in the bathroom, call the desk to borrow one.

A 52" x 70" tablecloth will make an extra long garment bag for formal dresses. Buy a sleeping bag zipper and trim off the excess zipper length to fit.

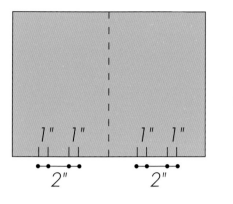

6   To prepare the place mat to make the back shoe pocket, fold place mat in half and mark the fold with pins. Make evenly spaced tucks in the lower edge of place mat as shown.

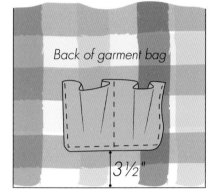

7   Topstitch center partition and three sides of shoe pocket to back of garment bag as shown.

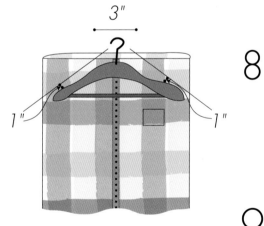

8   Turn garment bag inside out, centering zipper again. Lay wooden hanger centered at top. With a ruler, draw diagonal lines 1" above hanger as shown. Remove hanger. Stitch twice over drawn line. Trim seam allowances to 1". Serge or zigzag raw seam allowances. Turn bag right side out. Insert hanger.

9   Make bottom handle from the scraps trimmed off above hanger in step 8. Cut a piece of fabric 4" x 9" long. (This may have to be pieced to attain 9".) Press both long raw edges in to meet in the middle. Fold in half and topstitch all four edges. Pin ends of handle to bottom of bag between layers. Place ends of handle 4" apart.

10   Topstitch bottom of garment bag closed, topsitching over the tablecloth hems and enclosing bottom handle ends in this seam.

GALLERY

I hope you are inspired by the works of my friends, students and family. They often tell me they can no longer shop "normally", but end up folding, dreaming and visualizing purses made out of the most bizarre items. These ladies and I have an unspoken competition to see who can design something out of the most outrageous supplies!

Cheryl

I would love to see photos of your own designs! They may be sent to Homestead Specialties Pattern Company, Attn: Cheryl Weiderspahn, 1883 State Road, Cochranton, PA 16314.

"There is no beauty in art until it is shared. No magic until it is enjoyed. No meaning until it opens up our feelings for ourselves and our friends."
—Anonymous

A tapestry place mat cinched in with a chair tie.
← **By Marilyn Boyd**
(Cheryl's sister)

This purse is made from a bamboo bead place mat (that reminded us of piano keys) and a recorder makes an appropriate handle to "carry" the theme.
↑ **By Marilyn Boyd**

Purse and cosmetic bag made from two place mats
← ↓ **By Lauren Baker**

A beaded tote made from two beaded place mats and a potholder pocket.
↑ **By Karen Nowak**

A tote made from two tea towels.
↓ By Jean Cooper

A retro-looking purse made from two oval braided chair pads and a five-braid handle.
↑ By Opal Seber (Cheryl's mother)

This purse was made from a seasonal place mat and a coordinating potholder for a pocket.
By Becky Van Kleeck →

Using two round potholders, a tea towel, and beads and buttons produced this little purse.

By Suzanne Leonhart →

Khaki colored purse with shirred front flap and beaded handle. The body of the purse was made from one place mat.

↑ **By Sharon Madsen**

There's Been a Sighting, a tribute to Elvis Presley, is made from two pink place mats collaged with Elvis fabric, 1960s trims, and a real microphone, guitar pick and a 45 RPM record.

← **By Margie Hays**

A green faux suede and leather purse is trimmed with leopard ribbon made from one place mat.

↑ By Sharon Madsen

This ensemble includes a skirt, camisole and belt. The light blue handkerchief hem skirt is made from eight cloth napkins and the belt is five napkin rings and ribbon. The camisole is three white lace place mats.

↑ By Sharon Madsen

A blue/multi-colored embroidered drawstring bag with multi-colored fringed trim and ribbon handle. The bag was made from an embroidered place mat.

↑ By Sharon Madsen

A small tote pieced from a tea towel and other fabrics using rickrack for added decoration.
By Joan O'Donnell →

A mini purse or belt pack is made from a pocket potholder and necklace for the handle.
↓ By Cheryl Weiderspahn

With a coordinating potholder pocket, a place mat and matching napkin, this is a purse ready for the autumn season.
← By Marsha Waite

The Country Cottage Travel Set is a braided rug tote, eyeglasses case from a potholder, cosmetic bag (oval place mat), travel organizer (oval braided place mat) and a matching luggage tag.
↑ By Cheryl Weiderspahn

Tapestry drawstring purse with soap dish base.
↑ By Cheryl Weiderspahn

ABOUT THE AUTHOR

My original designs have been featured on the cover of Pfaff Club Magazine, in Lark Books, in Sew News, Sew Beautiful, Country Woman, Designs in Machine Embroidery, McCall's Quilting, Craftrends, Quick and Easy Crafts Magazines and in Creative Machine and Total Embellishment Newsletters. I have also appeared as a guest or guest host on Kay's Quilting Friends and Quilter's Toolbox TV shows as well as Quilter's News Network online. My patterns have been carried by many distributors and in over 600 U.S. shops and in several foreign countries.

RESOURCES

Annie's Attic
1 Annie Lane
Big Sandy, TX 75755
Phone: (800) 582-6643
Web: www.anniesattic.com

Around the Bend Patterns
*Unique dolls, backpacks, purses
and totes with character*
www.ruthprestdesigns.com
Phone: (814) 724-3668

Clotilde LLC
P.O. Box 7500
Big Sandy, TX 75755-7500
Phone: (800) 772-2891
Web: www.clotilde.com

Connecting Threads
P.O. Box 870760
Vancouver, WA 98687-7760
Phone: (800) 574-6454
Web: www.ConnectingThreads.com

Ghee's
2620 Centenary Blvd. No. 2-250
Shreveport, LA 71104
Phone: (318) 226-1701
E-mail: bags@ghees.com
Web: www.ghees.com

Herrschners, Inc.
2800 Hoover Road
Stevens Point, WI 54492-0001
Phone: (800) 441-0838
Web: www.herrschners.com

Home Sew
Sewing and craft supplies
P.O. Box 4099
Bethlehem, PA 18018-0099
Phone: (800) 344-4739
Web: www.homesew.com

Homestead Specialties Pattern Company
*Patterns by author Cheryl Weiderspahn-
designs with multiple wearing options and
unbelievable versatility. Unique closures,
hard-to-find notions and purse supplies*
www.homesteadspecialties.com
Phone: (814) 425-1183

Kaye Wood Inc.
*Quilters, Sewers, Home Decorators, and
wearable arts enthusiasts*
www.kayewood.com
Phone: (800) 248-KAYE (5293)

Keepsake Quilting
Route 25
P.O. Box 1618
Center Harbor, NH 03226-1618
Phone: (800) 438-5464
Web: www.keepsakequilting.com

Krause Publications
700 E. State St.
Iola, WI 54990
Phone: (800) 258-0929
Web: www.krausebooks.com

Lazy Girl Designs by Joan Hawley
*Patterns and products to make casual and
lighthearted purses and accessories*
www.lazygirldesigns.com
Phone: (800) 391-2867

Nancy's Notions
333 Beichl Ave.
P.O. Box 683
Beaver Dam, WI 53916-0683
Phone: (800) 833-0690
Web: www.nancysnotions.com

Newark Dressmaker Supply
Sewing and craft and dressmaking supplies
www.newarkdress.com
Phone: (800) 736-6783

HUNDREDS MORE LOW-SEW PROJECTS FOR YOUR WARDROBE AND HOME

Simple & Stylish Bead Accents
50+ Projects to Add Pizzazz to Gifts,
Fashions & Home Décor
by Katie Hacker

Featuring 50 easy-to-follow projects that can
be applied to fabric, wood, paper and plastic,
with technique instruction, beaders can create
beautiful beaded accents, including handbags,
wearables, picture frames, and much more.

Softcover • 8 ¼ x 10 ⅞ • 128 pages
100 color photos, 25+ illus.
Item# SSBA • $21.99

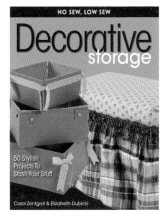

No Sew, Low Sew Decorative Storage
50 Stylish Projects to Stash Your Stuff
by Carol Zentgraf & Elizabeth Dubicki

This collection of 50 inexpensive and easy-to-
make storage solutions for the home can be
completed with a hot glue gun, basic hand
stitches, and other fast and easy techniques.
Includes step-by-step instructions and 150
illustrations.

Softcover • 8 ¼ x 10 ⅞ • 144 pages
100+ color photos, 50 illus.
Item# DECST • $24.99

No-Sew, Low-Sew Interior Décor
Instant Style Using Easy Techniques: Gluing,
Stapling, Fusing, Draping, Gathering
by Janis Bullis

Simply glue, staple, fuse, and stitch to create
fabulous "new" rooms. Includes shortcuts to
piping, pleating, quilting, and hemming, plus
more than 45 projects!

Softcover • 8 ¼ x 10 ⅞ • 128 pages
color throughout
Item# NSLSID • $19.95

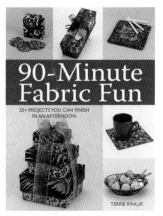

90-Minute Fabric Fun
30 Projects You Can Finish in an Afternoon
by Terrie Kralik

Create 30 beautiful projects for the home or
to give as gifts including fabric boxes and
bowls using fabric techniques explained and
demonstrated in 200 detailed color photos.

Softcover • 8 ¼ x 10 ⅞ • 144 pages
200+ color photos and illus.
Item# Z0102 • $24.99

Sew It In Minutes
24 Projects to Fit Your Style and Schedule
by Chris Malone

Provides instructions for 24 stylish projects that
can each be completed in four hours or less.
Projects include ornaments, photo frames,
appliquéd cloth bib and more.

Softcover • 8 ¼ x 10 ⅞ • 128 pages
175 color photos and illus.
Item# Z0133 • $22.99

Canvas Décor
25+ No-Sew, Low-Sew Projects for Your Home
by Bunny Delorie

Complete 30 inventive home décor projects
using inexpensive canvas! Includes step-by-step
photos and instructions for bamboo, palm tree,
Italian garden, outdoor, faux leather, animal fur
and children's room projects.

Softcover • 8 ¼ x 10 ⅞ • 144 pages
150 color photos
Item# CNVD • $22.99